I0438989

Characterization of Water Quality and Biological Communities, Fish Creek, Teton County, Wyoming, 2007–08

By Cheryl A. Eddy-Miller, David A. Peterson, Jerrod D. Wheeler, and Daniel J. Leemon

Prepared in cooperation with Teton Conservation District

Scientific Investigations Report 2010–5188

U.S. Department of the Interior
U.S. Geological Survey

U.S. Department of the Interior
KEN SALAZAR, Secretary

U.S. Geological Survey
Marcia K. McNutt, Director

U.S. Geological Survey, Reston, Virginia: 2010

For more information on the USGS—the Federal source for science about the Earth, its natural and living resources, natural hazards, and the environment, visit http://www.usgs.gov or call 1-888-ASK-USGS

For an overview of USGS information products, including maps, imagery, and publications, visit http://www.usgs.gov/pubprod

To order this and other USGS information products, visit http://store.usgs.gov

Contents

Figures

Tables

Conversion Factors

SI to Inch/Pound

Multiply	By	To obtain
Length		
centimeter (cm)	0.3937	inch (in.)
millimeter (mm)	0.03937	inch (in.)
meter (m)	3.281	foot (ft)
kilometer (km)	0.6214	mile (mi)
micrometer (μm)	0.000039	inch (in.)
Area		
square centimeter (cm^2)	0.001076	square foot (ft^2)
square meter (m^2)	10.76	square foot (ft^2)
square centimeter (cm^2)	0.1550	square inch (ft^2)
square kilometer (km^2)	0.386	square mile (mi^2)
Volume		
liter (L)	33.82	ounce, fluid (fl. oz)
cubic meter (m^3)	264.2	gallon (gal)
cubic meter (m^3)	35.31	cubic foot (ft^3)
cubic meter (m^3)	0.0008107	acre-foot (acre-ft)
Flow rate		
cubic meter per second (m^3/s)	70.07	acre-foot per day (acre-ft/d)
Mass		
gram (g)	0.03527	ounce, avoirdupois (oz)

Temperature in degrees Celsius (°C) may be converted to degrees Fahrenheit (°F) as follows:

$$°F=(1.8×°C)+32$$

Vertical coordinate information is referenced to the National Geodetic Vertical Datum of 1929 (NGVD 29).

Altitude, as used in this report, refers to distance above the vertical datum.

Horizontal coordinate information is referenced to the North American Datum of 1983 NAD 83).

Specific conductance is given in microsiemens per centimeter at 25 degrees Celsius (μS/cm at 25°C) or millisiemens per centimeter at 25 degrees Celsius (mS/cm at 25°C).

Concentrations of chemical constituents in water are given either in milligrams per liter (mg/L) or micrograms per liter (μg/L).

Stable isotope values of nitrogen and oxygen are referenced to a standard and are given in parts per thousand or per mil.

Abbreviations and initialisms used in this report

<	less than
cm^3/m^2	cubic centimeter per square meter
g/m^2	grams per square meter
mg/m^2	milligrams per square meter
AFDM	ash-free dry mass
AIR	atmospheric nitrogen
EPT	Ephemeroptera, Trichoptera, and Plecoptera
IDAS	Invertebrate Data Analysis System
LRL	laboratory reporting level
N	nitrogen
N:P	ratio of nitrogen to phosphorus concentrations
NMDS	nonmetric multidimensional scaling ordinations
NO_3	nitrate
NWQL	National Water Quality Laboratory
P	phosphorus
p	probability
P_{max}	maximum rate of productivity
PVC	polyvinyl chloride
r	correlation coefficient
RPS	rapid periphyton survey
RTH	richest-targeted habitat
ssp.	subspecies
USGS	U.S. Geological Survey
VSMOW	Vienna Standard Mean Ocean Water

Characterization of Water Quality and Biological Communities, Fish Creek, Teton County, Wyoming, 2007–08

By Cheryl A. Eddy-Miller,[1] David A. Peterson,[1] Jerrod D. Wheeler,[1] and Daniel J. Leemon[2]

Abstract

Fish Creek, a tributary to the Snake River, is about 25 river kilometers long and is located in Teton County in western Wyoming near the town of Wilson. Public concern about nuisance growths of aquatic plants in Fish Creek have been increasing in recent years. To address this concern, the U.S. Geological Survey conducted a study in cooperation with the Teton Conservation District to characterize the water quality and biological communities in Fish Creek. Water-quality samples were collected for analyses of physical properties and water chemistry (nutrients, nitrate isotopes, and wastewater chemicals) between March 2007 and October 2008 from seven surface-water sites and three groundwater wells. During this same period, aquatic plant and macroinvertebrate samples were collected and habitat characteristics were measured at the surface-water sites.

The main objectives of this study were to (1) evaluate nutrient concentrations (that influence biological indicators of eutrophication) and potential sources of nutrients by using stable isotope analysis and other indicator chemicals (such as caffeine and disinfectants) that could provide evidence of anthropogenic sources, such as wastewater or septic tank contamination in Fish Creek and adjacent groundwater, and (2) characterize the algal, macrophyte, and macroinvertebrate communities and habitat of Fish Creek.

Nitrate was the dominant species of dissolved nitrogen present in all samples and was the only bioavailable species detected at concentrations greater than the laboratory reporting level in all surface-water samples. Average concentrations of dissolved nitrate in surface water were largest in samples collected from the two sites with seasonal flow near Teton Village and decreased downstream; the smallest concentration was at downstream site A-Wck. Concentrations of dissolved nitrate in groundwater were consistently greater than concentrations in corresponding surface-water sites during the same sampling event. Orthophosphate was the primary dissolved species of phosphorus present in all surface-water and groundwater samples. The average concentration of dissolved orthophosphate in surface water was largest in samples collected from near Teton Village; samples from all other sites had similar average concentrations. Concentrations of dissolved orthophosphate in groundwater also were typically greater than concentrations in corresponding surface-water sites during the same sampling event.

The aquatic plant communities in Fish Creek typically were composed of a mixture of macrophytes, macroalgae, microalgae, and moss. The composition of the aquatic plant community in Fish Creek appeared to shift in the downstream direction in 2007. On average, the proportion of macrophytes ranged from about 1 percent at site A-R1U, the most upstream site, to 54 percent of the plant community at site A-R6D, the farthest downstream site sampled during 2007. The downstream increase in macrophytes was accompanied by a downstream decrease in microalgae. The average proportion of microalgae ranged from 80 percent at site A-R1U to 24 percent at site A-R6D. The proportion of the macroalgae *Cladophora* in the aquatic plant community was relatively high at sites A-Wck and A-R3D in both 2007 and 2008.

Concentrations of chlorophyll-*a*, which is one of the primary photosynthetic pigments in algal cells, tended to be higher at the sites with perennial flow than at sites with seasonal flow. Chlorophyll-*a* concentrations at the sites with perennial flow averaged more than 200 milligrams per square meter. Almost all of the chlorophyll-*a* concentrations from Fish Creek were in the range of, or exceeded, the range of 100 to 200 milligrams per square meter, which is suggested as an indicator of nuisance algal conditions by the U.S. Environmental Protection Agency.

Most of the 199 algal taxa identified in the 2007 samples were diatoms (Bacillariophyta), accounting for an average of 87 percent of the total taxa richness by sample. Blue-green algae composed about 8 percent of the taxa richness, and green algae (Chlorophyta) composed about 4 percent of the taxa richness, on average. In spite of having relatively few

[1] U.S. Geological Survey.
[2] Teton Conservation District.

species, blue-green algae commonly were dominant in terms of density (average of 47 percent), and green algae commonly were dominant in terms of biovolume (average of 68 percent) at sites with perennial flow. The taxonomic composition of the algal communities at sites with seasonal flow was notably different from the composition at sites with perennial flow.

Nitrogen-fixing algae were present and sometimes dominant in the algal communities of Fish Creek. Nitrogen-fixing algae include diatoms in the family Rhopalodiaceae and blue-green algae. Metrics for oxygen tolerance, organic nitrogen, and pollution class indicated relatively low organic enrichment in Fish Creek.

Similar to the algal communities, the macroinvertebrate taxa richness was lower at the sites with seasonal streamflow than at the sites farther downstream with perennial streamflow. The Diptera (true flies) composed about one-half of the macroinvertebrate taxa identified in Fish Creek. The Ephemeroptera (mayflies), Trichoptera (caddisflies), and Plecoptera (stoneflies), which are collectively known as the EPT, composed smaller proportions of the overall community taxa richness and were more common in May than August of both 2007 and 2008, indicating seasonal variation in community composition. Conversely, Diptera and noninsects accounted for higher proportions of the community taxa richness in August than May of both years. Although the seasonal change in macroinvertebrate community composition in Fish Creek indicates a shift toward more tolerant taxa later in the year, this change might be due to factors other than water quality, such as the change in algal communities.

Although nutrient concentrations in Fish Creek generally were low, the standing crop of algae in Fish Creek was high compared to other streams in the region and was within the range of nuisance conditions. This apparent paradox also has been noted in other ecosystems and can be explained by rapid consumption of nutrients by the aquatic community as soon as the nutrients are introduced to the system. Rapid consumption of nutrients might also be a factor in the lack of statistically significant correlation between nutrients (various forms of nitrogen and phosphorus) and algal standing crop (algal biovolume, algal cell density, and chlorophyll-*a*) in Fish Creek. Groundwater is a likely source of nutrient loading to Fish Creek based on substantial contributions of groundwater to Fish Creek and consistently higher concentrations of nutrients in the groundwater compared to the surface water. The aquatic plant communities in Fish Creek affect the macroinvertebrate and fish communities in various ways such as by providing food and shelter and by causing diel changes in dissolved oxygen. The seasonal changes in macroinvertebrate communities were consistent with the seasonal increases in *Cladophora* and macrophytes in Fish Creek that affect food and shelter available to the macroinvertebrates. The macroinvertebrates, in turn, are an important food source for the fish community that is dominated by salmonids, such as the Snake River cutthroat trout (*Oncorhynchus clarki* spp.).

Introduction

Fish Creek, an approximately 25-kilometer (km) long tributary to the Snake River, is located in Teton County in western Wyoming near the town of Wilson (fig. 1). Fish Creek is an important water body as it is used for irrigation, fishing, and recreation and adds scenic value to the Jackson Hole properties it runs through. The clear, cold water in Fish Creek makes it an important spawning tributary for the Snake River cutthroat trout (*Oncorhynchus clarki* spp. [Baxter and Stone, 1995]). The Fish Creek drainage is located along the southwestern margin of Jackson Hole. Fish Creek's drainage area includes part of the southern extent of the Teton Range and the southwestern part of Jackson Hole and is 183 square kilometers (km^2) at the U.S. Geological Survey (USGS) streamflow-gaging station, Fish Creek at Wilson, Wyoming (station 13016450; fig. 2) (Eddy-Miller and others, 2009). Groundwater and groundwater/surface-water interaction studies near Fish Creek have shown that streamflow in Fish Creek is very responsive to changes in groundwater levels, and flow in the creek is a combination of groundwater discharge to the stream as well as surface-water inflows from tributaries and irrigation diversion that terminate in Fish Creek (Nelson Engineering, 1992; Hinckley Consulting and Jorgensen Engineering, 1994; Wyoming State Engineer's Office; 2005, Eddy-Miller and others, 2009).

Public concern about nuisance growths of aquatic plants in Fish Creek has been increasing since the early 2000s (Brian Remlinger, Teton Conservation District, oral commun., 2004). Aquatic plants, such as algae and macrophytes, are integral parts of a healthy stream ecosystem because they are primary producers in the aquatic food web, providing food and habitat for invertebrates and other organisms. Excessive growths of aquatic plants, however, can be esthetically displeasing and a nuisance for anglers, irrigators, and other water users (Peterson and others, 2001). During daylight hours, aquatic plants produce oxygen that is essential for aquatic life, sometimes resulting in supersaturated concentrations of oxygen. At night, dissolved-oxygen concentrations can decrease to levels lethal to fish, particularly trout, because of microbial respiration and consumption of oxygen as a result of decomposition of plant cells and other organic matter in the water. Respiration and decomposition of organic matter consume oxygen throughout the day and night but are offset by photosynthesis during daylight hours.

To address concerns about nuisance algal growths in Fish Creek, the U.S. Geological Survey (USGS) conducted a study in cooperation with the Teton Conservation District to characterize the water quality and biological communities of Fish Creek. Water-quality samples were collected for analyses of physical properties and water chemistry between March 2007 and October 2008 from seven surface-water sites and three wells. During this same period, aquatic plant and macroinvertebrate samples were collected and habitat characteristics were measured at the seven surface-water sites. The main objectives

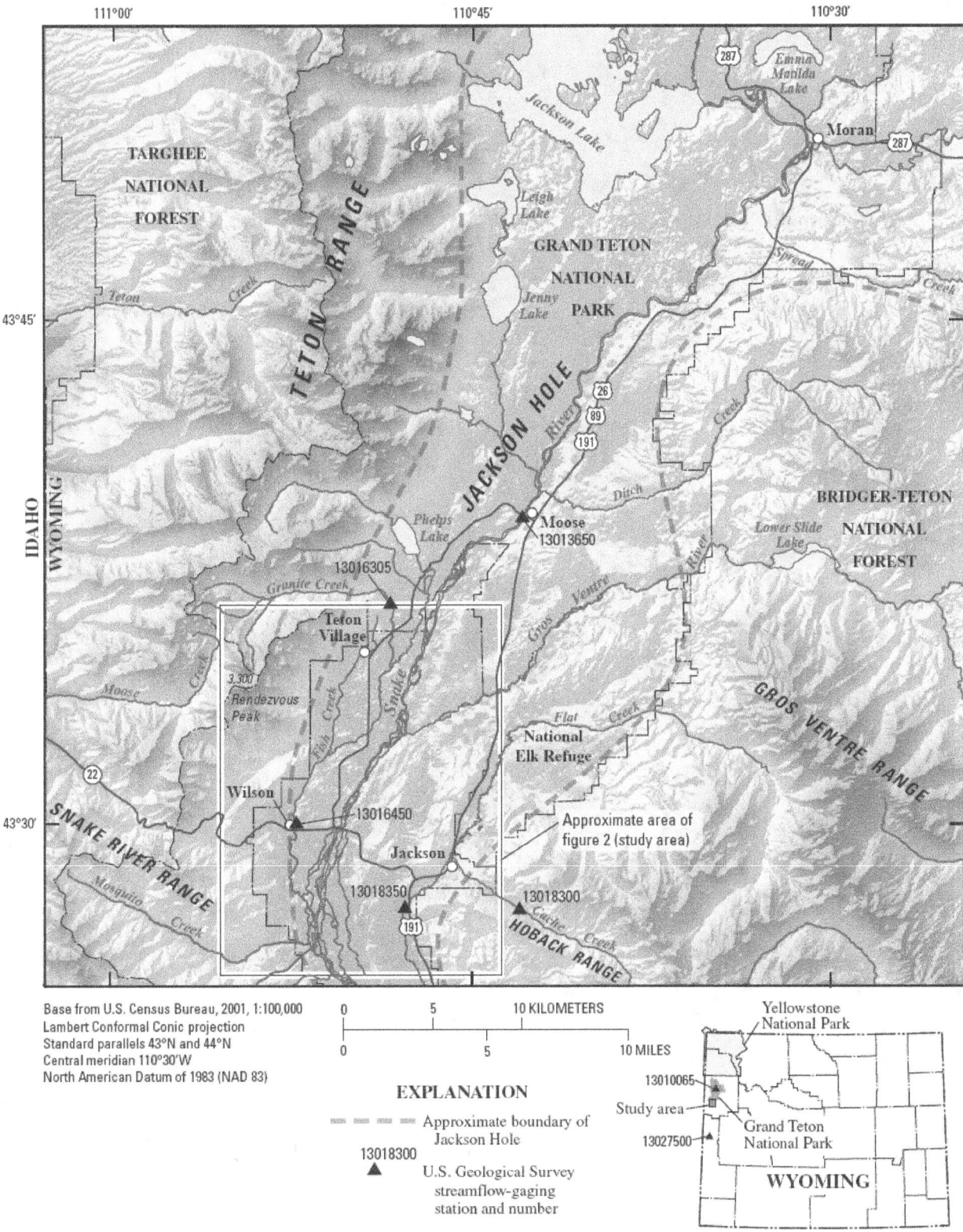

Figure 1. Location of Fish Creek study area as part of Jackson Hole.

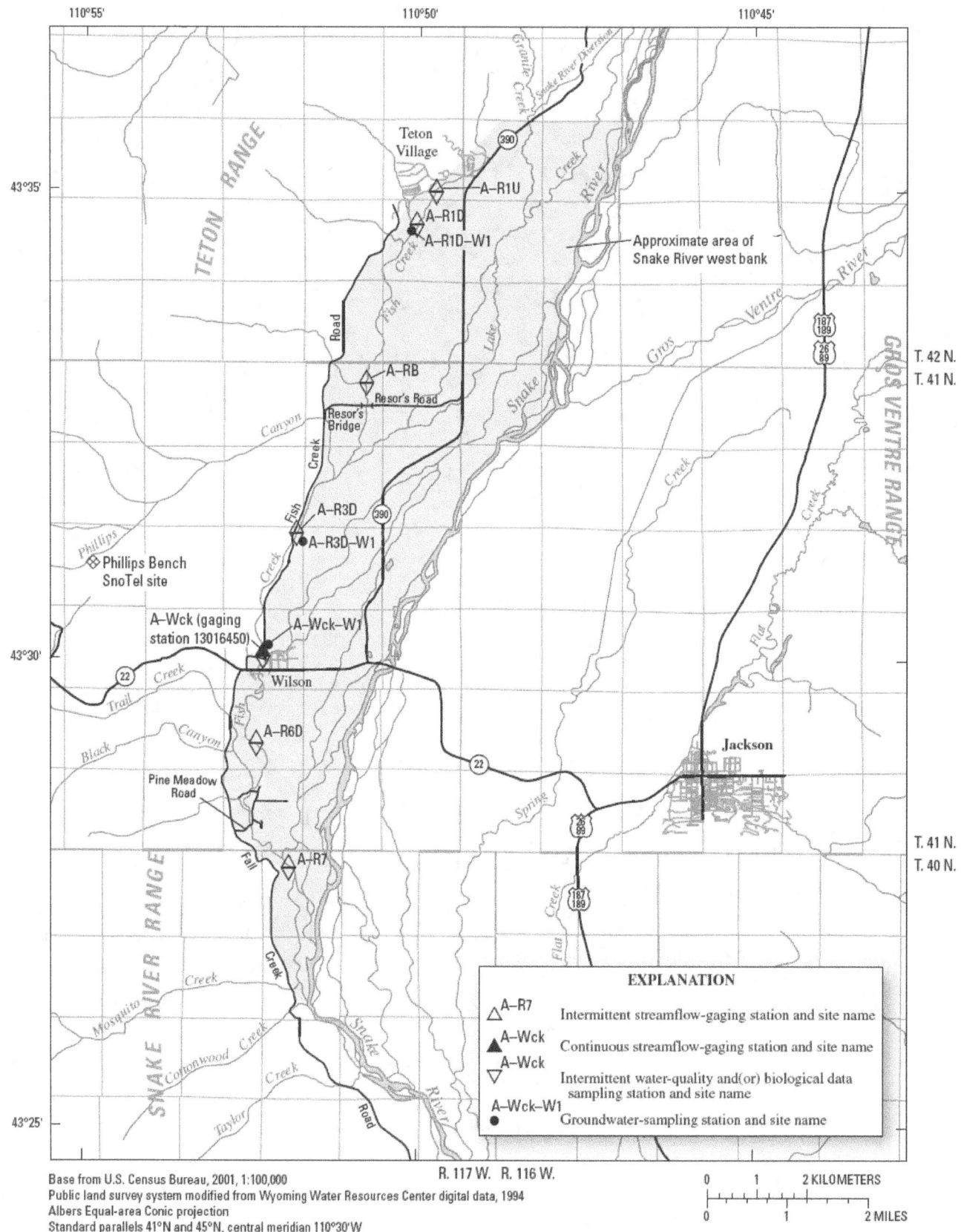

Figure 2.   Location of surface-water and groundwater sampling sites on and near Fish Creek, Wyoming.

of this study were to (1) evaluate nutrient concentrations (that influence biological indicators of eutrophication) and potential sources of nutrients by using stable isotope analysis and other indicator chemicals (such as caffeine and disinfectants) that could provide evidence of anthropogenic sources of contamination in Fish Creek and adjacent groundwater, and (2) characterize the algal, macrophyte, and macroinvertebrate communities and habitat of Fish Creek.

Purpose and Scope

The purpose of this report is to describe the characterization of water quality and biological communities of Fish Creek in western Wyoming using data collected during 2007–08. Physical properties were determined in the field for all surface-water and groundwater sites during each visit. Streamflow was measured at surface-water sites, and water-level data were collected at groundwater sites. Water-quality samples from Fish Creek and nearby groundwater were collected for analyses of nutrients, nitrate isotopes, and wastewater chemicals, depending on the sampling schedule. Biological samples (aquatic plants and macroinvertebrates) were collected and riparian canopy and pebble counts were measured at all surface-water sites.

Acknowledgments

The authors gratefully acknowledge the generous assistance of landowners near Fish Creek who provided access to their property for this study. Andrew Long, Nicholas Paretti, Janet Carter, and Mary Kidd, USGS, are acknowledged for their reviews of the draft. The authors also acknowledge assistance from Ty Blacklock, USGS, during the data-collection phase of the study, and Suzanne Roberts and Margo VanAlstine, USGS for publication assistance.

Description of Study Area

Teton County in Wyoming is experiencing rapid growth and development in the west bank area of the Snake River (fig. 2). Nelson Engineering (1992) estimated that 1,670 homes were in the west bank area in 1992. Between 1992 and 2007, an additional 640 homes were constructed in the west bank area (Jennifer Bodine, Teton County Planning and Development, written commun., 2008). Water is supplied to area residents from the alluvial aquifer, either from a water supply system or individual wells. Effluent from most of these residences and businesses is discharged into the alluvial aquifer through injection wells at a sewage-treatment plant or septic systems. The exception is effluent from the town of Wilson, which is piped to Jackson's waste disposal system. Multiple anthropogenic activities exist in the Fish Creek drainage basin including a ski area, golf courses, cattle grazing, and irrigation

associated with agricultural and esthetic uses that have the potential to affect water quantity and quality. Altitudes in the study area range from approximately 1,875 meters (m) above the National Geodetic Vertical Datum of 1929 (NGVD 29) at Fish Creek at the Wilson gaging station to about 3,200 m above the NGVD 29 at the summit of Rendezvous Peak.

Geology

The geology within the study area is structurally complex and is composed of diverse strata ranging from Precambrian-era basement rocks to Quaternary-era unconsolidated surficial deposits (fig. 3). The study area lies within the Jackson Hole, a folded and faulted downwarp of deposits 1,200 to 2,100 m thick, generally bounded by the Teton Range to the west and the anticlinal uplifts of the Gros Ventre and Washakie Ranges to the east (Nolan and Miller, 1995). The southern boundary of the basin consists of the Snake River, Hoback, and Salt River (not in fig. 1 map) Ranges associated with the Wyoming Thrust Belt (fig. l). The Teton Range is a north-south-trending, upthrown fault block that generally parallels the Fish Creek and Snake River drainages along the southern part of the valley. The associated Teton fault zone has caused westward tilting of the basin (fig. 3), which provides relief of nearly 1,500 m from the valley floor to the top of the peaks near the study area, and relief of more than 2,100 m in other parts of the valley.

The steep hillside of the Teton Range immediately west of Fish Creek consists of Precambrian-age metamorphosed (mafic) and other ultramafic rocks, granitic gneisses, and various granitic rocks with associated pegmatites (Love and others, 1992). Capping the Precambrian rocks are Paleozoic sedimentary sequences including the Flathead Sandstone, Gros Ventre Formation, Gallatin Limestone, Bighorn Dolomite, Darby Formation, and Madison Limestone (Love and others, 1992). Quaternary-age surficial deposits occupy most of the Fish Creek drainage basin and are primarily the result of glacial and postglacial fluvial deposition, both in the Snake River Basin and in some of the subsidiary tributary basins. Several areas of basin margin alluvial fans, flood-plain alluvium and colluvium, landslide debris, pediment, and talus deposits also exist in the area (Cox, 1974; Love and others, 1992).

The predominant surficial geology near Fish Creek between the Teton fault and the Snake River consists of an alluvial plain of unconsolidated clay, silt, sand, gravel, cobbles, and boulders that likely have high depositional variability and are highly permeable. These deposits include alluvium, colluvium, glacial till, and outwash as a result of fluvial deposition and Pleistocene-age valley glaciation (Nolan and Miller, 1995). Geophysical surveys have been performed in the area to attempt to determine the relative thickness of these Quaternary unconsolidated deposits. Results from a time-domain electromagnetic survey (Nolan and Miller, 1995) indicated that unconsolidated deposits range in thickness from 120 m to 730 m along the Jackson Hole valley, with a thickness

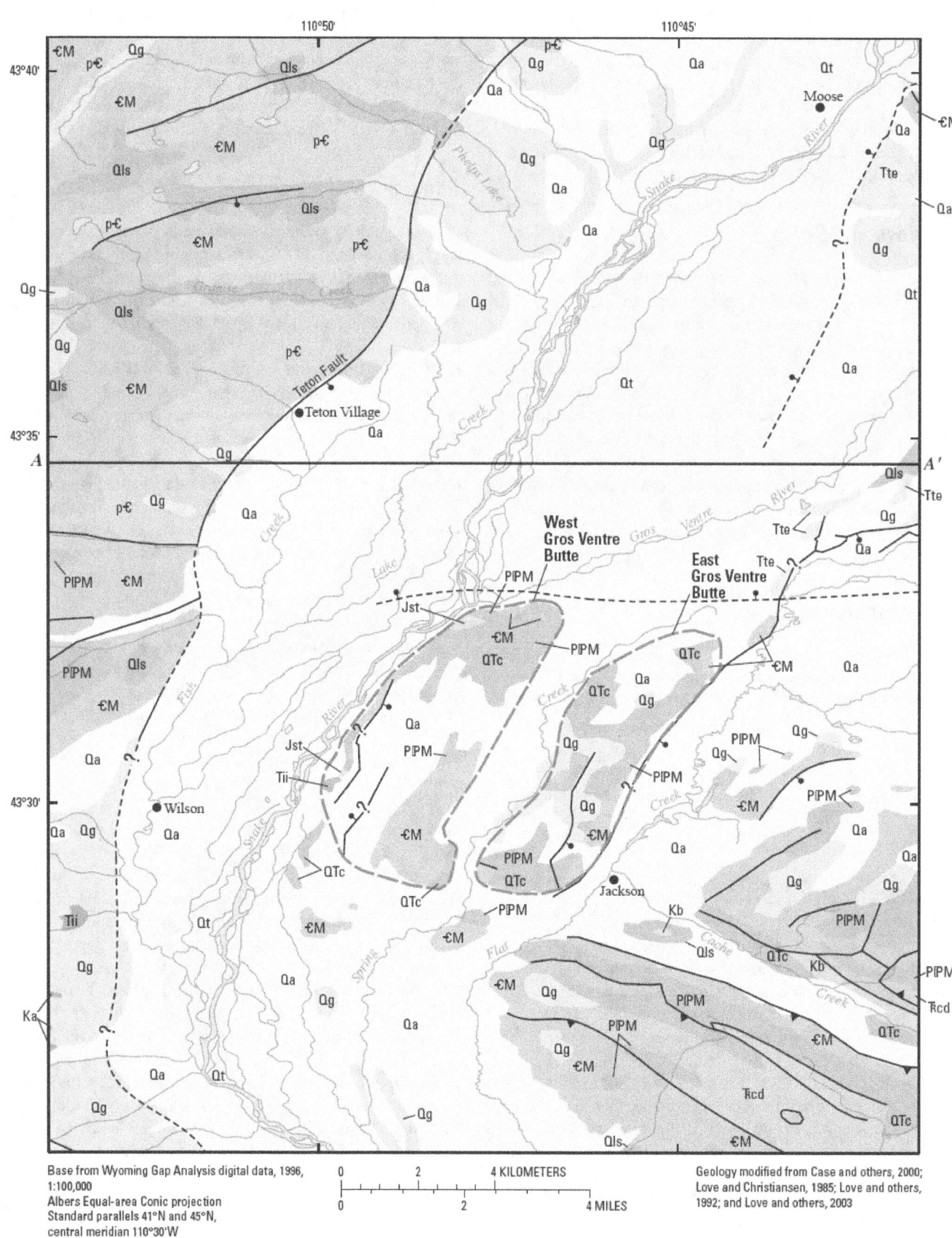

Figure 3.   Generalized geology and geologic section in the vicinity of Fish Creek.

EXPLANATION

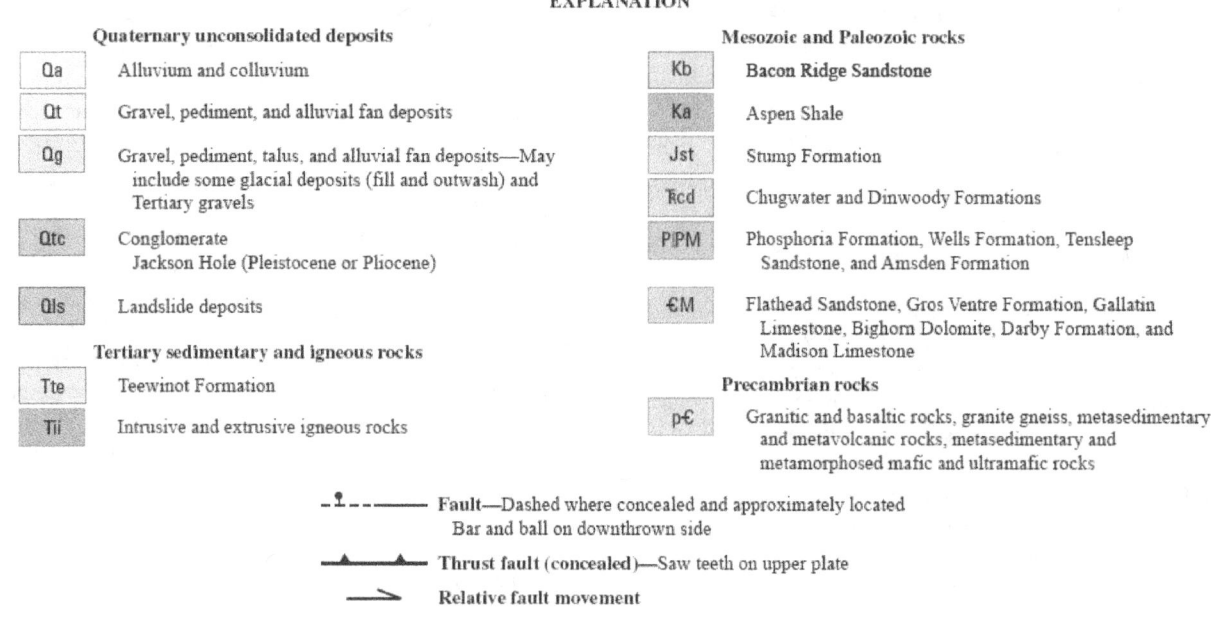

Quaternary unconsolidated deposits

Qa	Alluvium and colluvium
Qt	Gravel, pediment, and alluvial fan deposits
Qg	Gravel, pediment, talus, and alluvial fan deposits—May include some glacial deposits (fill and outwash) and Tertiary gravels
Qtc	Conglomerate Jackson Hole (Pleistocene or Pliocene)
Qls	Landslide deposits

Tertiary sedimentary and igneous rocks

Tte	Teewinot Formation
Tii	Intrusive and extrusive igneous rocks

Mesozoic and Paleozoic rocks

Kb	Bacon Ridge Sandstone
Ka	Aspen Shale
Jst	Stump Formation
Tcd	Chugwater and Dinwoody Formations
PIPM	Phosphoria Formation, Wells Formation, Tensleep Sandstone, and Amsden Formation
€M	Flathead Sandstone, Gros Ventre Formation, Gallatin Limestone, Bighorn Dolomite, Darby Formation, and Madison Limestone

Precambrian rocks

p€	Granitic and basaltic rocks, granite gneiss, metasedimentary and metavolcanic rocks, metasedimentary and metamorphosed mafic and ultramafic rocks

Fault—Dashed where concealed and approximately located Bar and ball on downthrown side

Thrust fault (concealed)—Saw teeth on upper plate

Relative fault movement

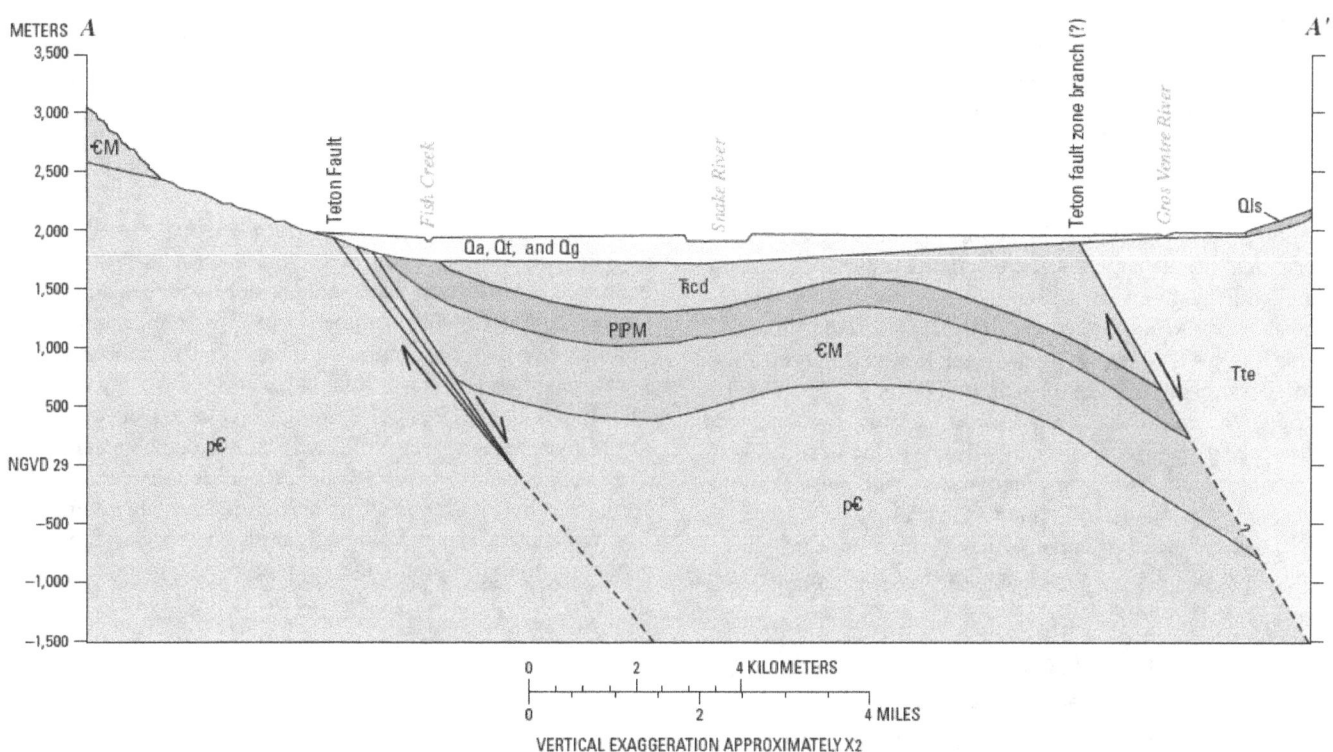

VERTICAL EXAGGERATION APPROXIMATELY X2

Details of fault and buried strata are approximate and largely diagrammatic. For simplicity, Quaternary-age deposits are not distinguished in the geologic section. Schematic based on a nearby cross section in Love and others (2003).

Figure 3. Generalized geology and geologic section in the vicinity of Fish Creek.—Continued

of 140 m near the confluence of the Gros Ventre River and Snake River. Results from an audio-magnetotellurics survey (Nolan and others, 1998), primarily conducted in the southern part of the valley and within the study area, indicated that unconsolidated material thickness ranged from 30 m in the southernmost part of the valley to 210 m near the town of Wilson. Groundwater velocities in the Quaternary unconsolidated deposits range from 1.1 to 5.5 m per day (Nelson Engineering, 1992).

Hydrology

On the west side of the Snake River is an alluvial aquifer known locally as the west bank aquifer that underlies the area shown as Snake River west bank in figure 2. The Fish Creek streambed is incised into the sediments of the Snake River alluvium and intersects the water table of the west bank aquifer. The water table in the west bank aquifer can rise due to natural recharge from precipitation on the valley floor, recharge from local flood irrigation, and injection of tertiary-treated sewage. The water table also rises from infiltration of recharge of water from Lake Creek, which has flow augmented by a diversion from the Snake River (Nelson Engineering, 1992), and from the Snake River, which is topographically higher in altitude than Fish Creek at a given latitude (Wyoming State Engineer's Office, 2005). Fish Creek surface-water inflows can include springs, irrigation diversions from area rivers and streams, irrigation return flows, and tributary streams. Groundwater discharge contributes a substantial portion of the flow to Fish Creek (Eddy-Miller and others, 2009), although the volume of water contributed from groundwater varies along the length of the creek.

Flow in Fish Creek in the area near Teton Village, the creek headwaters, is strongly influenced by two factors: (1) runoff from snowmelt directly upstream in the drainage basin and (2) the large fluctuations in the water table from applied irrigation water and an increased stage in the Snake River (Eddy-Miller and others, 2009). From Teton Village to near Resor's Bridge (fig. 2), the creek is seasonal, typically flowing from about late April through October. Near Resor's Bridge, the creek becomes perennial, and flow is influenced by increased groundwater discharge from a rising water table due to infiltration of valley snowmelt, a snowmelt pulse from the west-side mountains, infiltration of irrigation water application, and increased recharge from the higher stage of the Snake River to the west bank aquifer (Eddy-Miller and others, 2009). About 2 km downstream from Resor's Bridge, a major tributary, Lake Creek, enters Fish Creek. Flows in Fish Creek at Wilson are influenced in the summer by tributary inflows and a small, constant input of groundwater. Flows at Wilson in the winter have similar groundwater inputs, but the tributary inputs are minimal (Eddy-Miller and others, 2009).

Climate

The study area is semiarid with cold winters and warm summers. Average temperatures and annual precipitation are variable with changes in season and altitude. Average monthly temperatures at a climate station in Moose, Wyoming (fig. 1) ranged from −10.3 degrees Celsius (°C) in January to 16.0°C in July during the period 1958–2007 (National Climatic Data Center, 2009). Average temperatures decrease with increasing altitude. Total average precipitation near the study area, in the form of rain and snow, ranges annually from 54 centimeters (cm) at an altitude of 1,960 m above NGVD 29 near Moose, Wyo. (National Climatic Data Center, 2009) to more than 178 cm in the Teton Range at altitudes above 3,000 m (Oregon Climate Service, 2010). At the Phillips Bench SnoTel station (altitude of 2,500 m above NGVD 29) located about 4 km west, northwest of site A-Wck (fig. 2), the mean annual precipitation (1971–2000) was 112 cm (Natural Resources Conservation Service, 2008).

Methods of Study Design and Sample Collection

Seven surface-water and three groundwater sites were selected for sampling on the basis of their locations along the reach of Fish Creek from near the headwaters at Teton Village to a location about 2 km from the confluence with the Snake River (table 1, fig. 2). Surface-water and groundwater sites were sampled during 2007 and 2008 (table 2). Physical properties were determined in the field for all surface-water and groundwater sites during each visit. Streamflow was measured at surface-water sites, and water-level data were collected at groundwater sites. Water-quality properties of dissolved oxygen, pH, specific conductance, and water temperature were measured at all surface-water and groundwater sites during each visit. Water-quality samples from Fish Creek and nearby groundwater sites were collected for analyses of nutrients, nitrate isotopes, and wastewater chemicals, depending on the sampling schedule. Biological samples (aquatic plants and macroinvertebrates) were collected and habitat characteristics of streambed substrate (pebble count) and riparian canopy were measured at surface-water sites. Aquatic plant communities were surveyed and biological samples were analyzed for algae taxonomy, chlorophyll-*a*, and macroinvertebrate taxonomy. All samples were collected in accordance to published USGS or other protocols.

Table 1.   Sampling sites on and near Fish Creek, Teton County, Wyoming, 2007–08.

[S, seasonal; P, perennial; m³/s, cubic meters per second; n, number of measurements; na, not applicable]

Site name	Station number	Station name	Reach type	Well depth (meters)	Average instantaneous streamflow (m³/s)	Number of instantaneous flow measurements
		Surface-water sites				
A-R1U	433505110494001	Fish Creek, nr headwaters, south of Teton Village, WY	S	na	0.05	3
A-R1D	433438110495901	Fish Creek about 1 mile south of Teton Village, WY	S	na	.65	4
A-RB	433302110504701	Fish Creek 1/2 mile above Resor's Bridge	P	na	1.60	8
A-R3D	433117110515101	Fish Creek about 1.5 miles north of Wilson, WY	P	na	5.57	8
A-Wck	13016450	Fish Creek at Wilson, WY	P	na	5.74	8
A-R6D	432906110522601	Fish Creek about 1 mile south of Wilson, WY	P	na	6.26	8
A-R7	432748110515301	Fish Creek at Crescent H Ranch, near Wilson, WY	P	na	6.78	3
		Groundwater sites				
A-R1D-W1	433431110501101	42-117-25bcd01	na	2.59	0.84	5
A-R3D-W1	433122110514201	41-117-15aaa01	na	2.68	.95	5
A-Wck-W1	433005110521801	41-117-22dbb07	na	2.47	.71	6

Study Design

Six surface-water sites, A-R1U, A-R1D, A-RB, A-R3D, A-Wck, and A-R6D (fig. 2) and three newly installed monitoring wells, A-R1D-W1, A-R3D-W1, and A-Wck-W1(fig. 2) were sampled during 2007. These initial sites were selected, in part, to relate sampling results to a seepage investigation (Wheeler and Eddy-Miller, 2005) and a groundwater/surface-water interaction study (Eddy-Miller and others, 2009) of Fish Creek. During the 2008 sampling season, sites A-R1U and A-R1D were discontinued as sampling sites for the full set of analyses, although A-R1D remained as a water-quality sampling site, and site A-R7 (fig. 2) was added as a sampling site.

Site A-R1U is near the headwaters of the stream and is the most upstream location where Fish Creek has a defined channel. Site A-R1D is at the downstream end of the rechannelized section of the stream in the Teton Village area. Previous studies showed that Fish Creek rapidly gains flow from groundwater input between these two sites (Wheeler and Eddy-Miller, 2005; Eddy-Miller and others, 2009).

Four sites on Fish Creek with perennial flow were selected and sampled during both 2007 and 2008 (table 2). Site A-RB is located near the location where Fish Creek transitions from a seasonal to a perennial stream. Site A-R3D was part of the seepage investigation, and is the first site downstream from the Lake Creek tributary input. Site A-Wck is at USGS gaging

station 13016450. The colocation of this site with the gaging station was important for relating the data collected during this study to the long-term hydrologic data collected at the station. Initially, site A-R6D was selected as the most downstream site sampled, the same as for the seepage investigation.

The seasonal nature of flow at sites A-R1U and A-R1D, local interest in sites farther downstream from A-R6D, and budget constraints prompted a change in sites and analyses for the 2008 season (table 2). Most of the sample collection and analyses were discontinued for sites A-R1U and A-R1D in order to quantify the characteristics of the entire perennial part of the stream. Site A-R1D was still sampled for physical properties and nutrients to evaluate differences in groundwater and surface-water nutrient concentrations in the colocated well, A-R1D-W1. Site A-R7 was established in 2008 to characterize Fish Creek at a location closer to its confluence with the Snake River.

Three shallow (about 2.5 m below land surface), small-diameter (2 cm) PVC wells with 1.5-m screens were installed in March and May of 2007. The wells were installed by pounding a 3-cm diameter steel pipe with disposable well point into the ground, inserting the screened 2-cm well inside, then extracting the steel pipe. Each well was located between 10 and 160 m away from the stream in the estimated upstream groundwater flow path of one of the surface-water sampling sites.

Table 2.   Sampling schedule for analyses of physical properties, water chemistry, aquatic plants, macroinvertebrates, and habitat, Fish Creek, Wyoming, 2007–08.

[D, dry; Q, streamflow; CQW,[1] continuous water quality; WL, water level; IQW,[1] instantaneous water quality; Ch, chlorophyll-*a*; AT, algal taxonomy; RPS, rapid periphyton survey; N, nutrients; NI, nitrate isotopes; WW, wastewater chemicals; EF, equipment failure; M, macroinvertebrate classification; RS, ruined sample; PC, pebble count; RC, riparian canopy; --, no sample scheduled or attempted]

Sampling types	Surface-water sites							Groundwater sites		
	A-R1U	A-R1D	A-RB	A-R3D	A-Wck	A-R6D	A-R7	A-R1D-W1	A-R3D-W1	A-Wck-W1
March 2007										
Physical properties	D	D	Q CQW	Q CQW	Q CQW	Q CQW	--	D	WL IQW	WL IQW
Water chemistry	D	D	N NI WW	N NI WW	N WW	N NI WW	--	D	N NI WW	N NI WW
Aquatic plants	D	D	Ch AT RPS	Ch AT RPS	Ch AT RPS	Ch AT RPS	--	D	--	--
May 2007										
Physical properties	Q CQW	D	Q CQW	Q CQW	Q EF	Q CQW	--	WL IQW	WL IQW	WL IQW
Water chemistry	N NI WW	D	N NI WW	N NI WW	N WW	N NI WW	--	N NI WW	N NI WW	N NI WW
Aquatic plants	Ch AT	D	Ch AT RPS	Ch AT RPS	Ch AT RPS	Ch AT RPS	--	--	--	--
Macroinvertebrates	M	D	M	M	M	M	--	--	--	--
July 2007										
Physical properties	Q CQW	Q CQW	Q CQW	Q CQW	Q CQW	Q CQW	--	--	--	--
Aquatic plants	Ch AT RPS	Ch AT RPS	Ch AT RPS	Ch AT RPS	Ch AT RPS	Ch AT RPS	--	--	--	--
August 2007										
Physical properties	Q CQW	Q CQW	Q CQW	Q CQW	Q CQW	Q CQW	--	WL IQW	WL IQW	WL IQW
Water chemistry	--	--	N NI WW	N WW	N WW	N WW	--	N NI WW	N NI WW	N NI WW
Aquatic plants	Ch AT RPS	Ch AT RPS	Ch AT RPS	Ch AT RPS	Ch AT RPS	Ch AT RPS	--	--	--	--
Macroinvertebrates	M	M	M	M	M	M	--	--	--	--

Table 2.   Sampling schedule for analyses of physical properties, water chemistry, aquatic plants, macroinvertebrates, and habitat, Fish Creek, Wyoming, 2007–08.—Continued

[D, dry; Q, streamflow; CQW,[1] continuous water quality; WL, water level; IQW,[1] instantaneous water quality; Ch, chlorophyll-*a*; AT, algal taxonomy; RPS, rapid periphyton survey; N, nutrients; NI, nitrate isotopes; WW, wastewater chemicals; EF, equipment failure; M, macroinvertebrate classification; RS, ruined sample; PC, pebble count; RC, riparian canopy; --, no sample scheduled or attempted]

Sampling types	Surface-water sites							Groundwater sites		
	A-R1U	A-R1D	A-RB	A-R3D	A-Wck	A-R6D	A-R7	A-R1D-W1	A-R3D-W1	A-Wck-W1
October 2007										
Physical properties	D	D	Q CQW	Q CQW	Q CQW	Q CQW	--	--	--	--
Aquatic plants	D	D	Ch AT RPS	Ch AT RPS	Ch AT RPS	Ch AT RPS	--	--	--	--
May 2008										
Physical properties	--	D	Q CQW	Q CQW	Q CQW	Q CQW	Q CQW	WL IQW	WL IQW	WL IQW
Water chemistry	--	D	N	N	N	N	N	N	N	N
Aquatic plants	--	D	Ch RPS	Ch RPS	Ch RPS	Ch RPS	Ch RPS	--	--	--
Macroinvertebrates	--	D	M	M	M	M	M	--	--	--
Habitat	--	D	PC	PC	PC	PC	PC	--	--	--
August 2008										
Physical properties	--	Q IQW	Q QWC	Q CQW	Q CQW	Q CQW	Q CQW	WL IQW	WL IQW	WL IQW
Water chemistry	--	N	RS	N	N	N	N	N	N	N
Aquatic plants	--	--	Ch RPS	Ch RPS	Ch RPS	Ch RPS	Ch RPS	--	--	--
Macroinvertebrates	--	--	M	M	M	M	M	--	--	--
October 2008										
Physical properties	--	Q	Q CQW	Q CQW	Q CQW	Q CQW	Q CQW	WL IQW	WL IQW	WL IQW
Water chemistry	--	N	N	RS	N	N	N	N	N	N
Aquatic plants	--	--	Ch RPS	Ch RPS	Ch RPS	Ch RPS	Ch RPS	--	--	--
Habitat	--	--	PC RC	PC RC	PC RC	PC RC	PC RC	--	--	--

[1]Continuous and instantaneous water quality includes dissolved oxygen, pH, specific conductance, and water temperature.

Physical Properties

Onsite measurements of physical properties of streamflow, water levels, and water-quality properties were made using standard methods described in Rantz and others (1982), Sauer (2002), and Koterba (1998). Streamflow or water level, depending on the type of site, was measured each time the site was visited (table 2). Streamflow is noted as estimated if the measurement rating was considered poor.

Water-quality properties of dissolved oxygen, pH, specific conductance, and water temperature were measured with a multiprobe instrument either continuously or instantaneously according to methods described in the National Field Manual for the Collection of Water-Quality Data (U.S. Geological Survey, variously dated). Continuous measurements were recorded every 15 minutes at sites where chlorophyll-*a* data were collected for a minimum of 48 hours to record diel (24-hour period) fluctuations. Instantaneous measurements were collected in wells, after the removal of at least three well volumes of standing water (USGS, variously dated), and in the stream when water chemistry samples were being collected. Air temperatures were noted as estimated when non-NIST-checked thermometers were used to obtain the values.

Water Chemistry

Water samples were collected for analysis of nutrients (nitrogen and phosphorus species), isotopes of nitrate, and wastewater chemicals (table 10 in the "Supplemental Data" section) from surface-water and groundwater sites. Surface-water samples were collected with depth-integrating samplers at equal intervals across the stream according to USGS standard methods (U.S. Geological Survey, variously dated). Samples were composited in a Teflon churn splitter. Bottles were filled with unfiltered water for selected total nutrient analyses, water filtered through a 0.45-micrometer (μm) capsule filter for selected dissolved nutrient analyses and for nitrate isotope analyses, or water filtered through a 0.70-μm glass-fiber filter for wastewater chemical analyses, then preserved and shipped according to USGS standard methods. Groundwater samples were collected with Teflon equipment by using methods described in Koterba (1998), and processed the same as the surface-water samples.

Samples to be analyzed for nutrients were shipped to the USGS National Water Quality Laboratory (NWQL) in Lakewood, Colorado. Nutrients were analyzed using methods described in Patton and Kryskalla (2003) and Fishman (1993). Filtered samples were analyzed for dissolved ammonia, nitrate plus nitrite, nitrite, orthophosphate, and total dissolved nitrogen (analytically determined total of dissolved nitrate, nitrite, ammonia, and organic nitrogen), and total dissolved phosphorus (analytically determined total of all forms of dissolved phosphorus). Unfiltered samples were analyzed for total nitrogen (analytically determined total of total nitrate, nitrite, ammonia, and organic nitrogen) and total phosphorus (analytically determined total of all forms of total phosphorus). Analysis of the isotopes of nitrate requires nitrate presence in the sample. Therefore, after results of nutrient analyses were obtained from NWQL, samples with sufficient nitrate were selected to be shipped to the Reston Stable Isotope Laboratory for analysis (Sigman and others, 2001; Casciotti and others, 2002; Révész and Casciotti, 2007).

Wastewater chemicals are a set of compounds found in water affected by anthropogenic activities. This suite of chemicals consists of pesticides, fragrances, flavorings, cosmetics, pharmaceuticals, human metabolites of parent compounds (nicotine, caffeine, and menthol), and petroleum products (table 10). The detection of any of these compounds can indicate anthropogenic effects in a drainage basin. Samples for wastewater chemical analyses were shipped to the USGS NWQL. The analytical methods for wastewater chemical determination used solid-phase extraction and capillary-column gas-chromatography/mass spectrometry described in Zaugg and others (2002). Table 10 lists all chemicals, their uses, and the laboratory reporting level (LRL) for wastewater chemicals analyzed for this study. The LRL generally is equal to twice the yearly determined long-term method detection level (Childress and others, 1999). Concentrations commonly are estimated when the concentration is greater than the minimum reporting level (MRL), defined by the NWQL as the smallest measured concentration of a substance that can be reliably measured by using a given analytical method (Timme, 1995), but less than the LRL. Generally, concentrations that are less than the LRL have more uncertainty in their quantification than concentrations larger than LRLs.

Aquatic Plants

Aquatic plant communities were surveyed at surface-water sites to estimate the relative proportion of macrophytes, moss, macroalgae, and microalgae present, following procedures modified from Barbour and others (1999, p. 6–21 to 6–23) noted as RPS (rapid periphyton survey). At each site, three transects were established across the stream near the location of the algae and macroinvertebrate sampling. Three points were then randomly selected along each transect, and a viewing bucket with a 50-dot grid was used to record the type of aquatic plants present at a total of about 450 points per site on each sampling date. The plant types classified were macrophytes, which generally are large aquatic submergent plants with distinct stems and leaves; moss, which was true aquatic moss (Bryophyta); macroalgae, which includes the filamentous green algae *Cladophora* (Chlorophyta) and the colonial blue-green algae (cyanobacteria) *Nostoc* (Cyanophyta); and microalgae, which is the thin film (generally less than 5 millimeters (mm) thick) of algae such as diatoms present on the substrate. In cases where the substrate was judged to be too small or unstable to support growths of filamentous algae (fine gravel or smaller), the point was recorded as unsuitable substrate. Transects generally were laid out across the stream, perpendicular to the flow, except at site A-R1U where the narrow channel was surveyed with a transect parallel to the flow. Sites A-R1U and A-R1D were surveyed with the RPS bucket procedure only in July and August 2007 because of the seasonal flow at those sites. The other sites, A-RB, A-R3D, A-Wck, and A-R6D, where perennial flow exists, were surveyed five times in 2007, (March, May, July, August, and October) and three times in 2008 (May, August, and October; table 2). Consistent with the overall study design, sites A-R1U and A-R1D were not sampled in 2008, and one site, A-R7 (fig. 2), was added for the 2008 sampling. Samples of the dominant macrophytes were collected from selected sites during May and August, 2007, and sent to Burrell E. (Ernie) Nelson of the Rocky Mountain Herbarium at the University of Wyoming in Laramie for taxonomic identification.

The algal communities sampled in Fish Creek were the periphyton, or algae, attached to rocks in riffles. The protocol used, as described by Moulton and others (2002), was to collect periphyton from 25 rocks using a cylindrical delimiter and brush when the algae were primarily present as a film, or to collect periphyton using a top-rock scrape method when the algae were present primarily as branched filaments. Algal samples were homogenized before aliquots were filtered, preserved on dry ice, and sent to the USGS NWQL for analysis of chlorophyll-a and ash-free dry mass (AFDM). Separate aliquots were preserved with formalin and sent to the Academy of Natural Sciences in Philadelphia, Pa., for taxonomic identification and enumeration following the NAWQA protocol (Charles and others, 2002). Quality control (QC) samples for chlorophyll-a, AFDM, and algal taxonomy were collected as splits at site A-R1U in July and site A-R6D in October and analyzed by the same methods used for environmental samples.

Algal community traits were calculated using algal autecology attributes described by Porter (2008). Tolerance and trophic metrics were calculated from all taxa, whereas Van Dam metrics (Van Dam and others, 1994) were calculated from diatoms only. Ambiguous taxa were resolved by distributing parents among children using the Algal Data Analysis System (Thomas F. Cuffney, U.S. Geological Survey, written commun., June 17, 2008). The PRIMER software (Clarke and Gorley, 2006) was used to calculate Bray-Curtis similarity coefficients (Bray and Curtis, 1957), which measure taxonomic (dis-)similarity among samples. The PRIMER software also was used to prepare nonmetric multidimensional scaling ordinations (NMDS), which show taxonomic similarities among sites on the basis of the Bray-Curtis coefficients. Algal and macroinvertebrate abundance data were log-transformed ($\log x + 1$) to approximate normality before statistical tests were performed, except as indicated for linear Pearson correlation coefficients (r) and associated significance level (p) (Clarke and Gorley, 2006). Values of r generally can range from 0.00 (no correlation) to 1.00 (complete correlation) and were considered significant at $p < 0.05$.

Macroinvertebrate Communities

Macroinvertebrate samples were collected in the richest-targeted habitat (RTH) following protocols described in Moulton and others (2002). RTH samples are intended to represent the habitat with highest taxa richness. Each RTH macroinvertebrate sample was a composite of five 0.25-square-meter (m^2) samples collected from multiple riffles, where available, with a Slack sampler equipped with 500-μm mesh. Macroinvertebrate samples were sent to Richard Durfee, formerly with RD Aquatics, in Pueblo West, Colo., for taxonomic identification and enumeration. A minimum of 500 macroinvertebrates were analyzed per sample and identified to genus or species for insects and higher levels for noninsects as appropriate. A reference collection of identified macroinvertebrates is maintained by the Teton Conservation District. Ambiguous taxa were resolved by distributing parents among children by using the Invertebrate Data Analysis System (IDAS) (Cuffney, 2003). IDAS also was used to calculate macroinvertebrate metrics. Macroinvertebrate abundance data were log-transformed ($\log x + 1$) to approximate normality before Bray-Curtis similarity coefficients and NMDS ordinations of the macroinvertebrate taxonomic data were analyzed using PRIMER (Clarke and Gorley, 2006), similar to the methods described for the algal data analysis.

Habitat Characteristics

Habitat characteristics that were measured at surface-water sites for this study were streambed substrate (pebble counts) and riparian canopy. Pebble counts were measured according to Wolman (1954) in May and October of 2008, with a minimum of 100 particles measured along transects at each site. Particle sizes were categorized according to Potyondy and Bunte (2002). Densiometer readings to assess the variability and influence of the riparian canopy on Fish Creek were collected according to Fitzpatrick and others (1998) on the right and left banks at three transects for each site sampled in October 2008.

Water-Quality Characterizations

The physical properties measured at and water chemistry samples analyzed from the seven surface-water and three groundwater sites help characterize the water quality of Fish Creek from the upper part of the stream near the headwaters, to the most downstream site near its confluence with the Snake River. The sampling schedule during spring, summer, and fall helped to characterize seasonal characteristics of the creek. Water-quality results are compared to results of studies of nearby water bodies and to applicable water-quality standards.

Physical Properties

Field measurements of physical properties of streamflow, groundwater level, and water-quality properties (dissolved oxygen, pH, specific conductance, and water temperature) characterize the physical nature of Fish Creek. Streamflow or groundwater levels and water-quality properties were measured each time a site was visited. In addition, water-quality properties were continuously monitored at selected surface-water sites.

Streamflow

Instantaneous streamflow measurements that were made during collection of water-quality samples at surface-water sites are shown in table 3 and figure 4. Streamflow ranged from 0.04 cubic meter per second (m^3/s) to 11 m^3/s, indicating that water-quality samples were collected during a wide range of hydrologic conditions.

Streamflow in Fish Creek is affected by groundwater inflow, snowmelt runoff, tributary inflow, irrigation diversions, and irrigation return flows. Streamflow at the streamflow-gaging station at Wilson (13016450) has been continuously measured since March 1994 (U.S. Geological Survey, 2010a). During base-flow conditions, flow at the gaging station is about 1.1 m^3/s, and during mid-May to mid-July flow typically is greater than 14 m^3/s (Wheeler and Eddy-Miller, 2005; fig. 4), with peak flows as great as 40.5 m^3/s, occurring in 1997 (fig. 5). The average annual mean daily flow at Wilson, during the 15 years of annual statistical calculations (water years 1995–2009), was 5.3 m^3/s (U.S. Geological Survey, 2009). The average annual mean daily flow in water year 2007 was the same as the 15-year average of 5.3 m^3/s. The average annual mean daily flow in water year 2008 of 5.6 m^3/s was slightly higher than the 15-year average. In addition, the total volume of flow passing by the gaging station, measured in cubic meters (m^3) of annual runoff, was near average in 2007 and was slightly higher in 2008 than the mean annual runoff for the previous 15 years of streamflow record. Annual runoff for 2007 and 2008 was 1.67×10^8 m^3 and 1.76×10^8 m^3, respectively, with the 15-year average annual runoff at 1.65×10^8 m^3.

Average mean daily streamflow as plotted on an annual basis shows the variability between Fish Creek and other streamflow-gaging stations in the Jackson Hole valley (fig. 6). When compared with other drainages in the valley, Fish Creek exhibits a streamflow pattern more similar to that of the larger Snake River system than to those of drainages closer to Fish Creek's size and characteristics, largely due to the influence of both groundwater and surface-water inputs from the Snake River. Gaging stations on Granite Creek and Cache Creek, both with similar drainage areas, show streamflows that are more typical of an unregulated snowmelt-driven system, with groundwater-induced base flow most of the year, augmented by a sharp increase in May, peak flows in June–July, and a return to base-flow conditions by the end of August. In contrast, Fish Creek has an annually consistent increase that is earlier, beginning in late March through April, as lowland valley snowmelt occurs, some irrigation in the west bank area begins, and seasonal releases from Jackson Lake cause increases in stage to occur in the Snake River, subsequently recharging the west bank aquifer that discharges to Fish Creek. This early rise is followed by snowmelt runoff peak flows in late May–July, which are on average four times greater than peak flows for Flat Creek, a quasi-regulated drainage of similar size located across the valley. As peak flows subside in mid-August, Fish Creek shows a more gradual recession through the end of September, as the raised groundwater table (from irrigation infiltration and raised Snake River stage) discharges to the creek and irrigation return flows terminate in the creek. As the irrigation season abruptly ends near the beginning of October, a sharp decrease in flow occurs, likely from quickly receding surface-water inputs as evidenced by the sharp drop inflows in the Snake River. Flows in Fish Creek continue a more gradual recession to base-flow conditions in late November than that of the Snake River, the result of a slow recession of groundwater input to the system.

Groundwater Levels

Groundwater-level measurements that were made during collection of water-quality samples at monitoring wells are shown in table 4. Measured water levels indicate the groundwater level is less dynamic in the lower reaches of Fish Creek at sites A-R3D-W1 and A-Wck-W1 than in the headwaters near Teton Village at site A-R1D-W1 (table 4). The water levels in wells A-R3D-W1 and A-Wck-W1 changed about 0.4 m between the time of low and high water tables. The water table in well A-R1D-W1 changed more than 2.3 m (the depth of the well), as the water level near well A-R1D-W1 was lower than the bottom of the well during the time of low water table. These results are similar to those found in Eddy-Miller and others (2009), Nolan and Miller (1995), and Nelson Engineering (1992).

Water-Quality Properties

Water-quality properties, continuous or instantaneous, were measured during each sampling event. Water-quality properties that were measured include dissolved oxygen, pH, specific conductance, and water temperature. Instantaneous water-quality properties are listed in table 3 for the surface-water sites and in table 4 for the groundwater sites; instantaneous measurements also can be accessed at *http://nwis.waterdata.usgs.gov/wy/nwis/qwdata*. Continuously collected data for the surface-water sites are in tables 11–18 in the "Supplemental Data" included on the CD–ROM. Continuously collected data for August 2008 are displayed in figure 7 as an example, and in figures 28–34 in the "Supplemental Data" section for the other sampling dates (table 2).

Continuous water-quality data show patterns that are evident in many of the sets of diel data. For example, in August 2008 (fig. 7), water temperature has a different pattern at site A-RB than at the downstream sites. Site A-RB has a lower volume of flow (table 3), which requires less time to heat up throughout the day. The water temperature at this site also remains warmer at night compared to the downstream sites and has a smaller temperature fluctuation in a 24-hour period, indicating a larger part of the creek's water is from ground-water in the headwater area near site A-RB. The larger volume of flow at site A-R3D and farther downstream sites lead to more similar water-quality properties when compared to site A-RB.

Water Chemistry

Samples were collected from Fish Creek and nearby groundwater sites and analyzed for nutrients, isotopes of nitrate, and wastewater chemicals. Dissolved concentrations of ammonia, nitrate, nitrite, orthophosphate, total nitrogen (sum of dissolved nitrate, nitrite, ammonia, and organic nitrogen), and total phosphorus (sum of dissolved species) were determined. Total concentrations (unfiltered samples) were determined for total nitrogen (sum of total nitrate, nitrite, ammonia, and organic nitrogen) and total phosphorus (sum of species). The isotopes of nitrate were analyzed as they can help identify the sources of nitrate detected. Wastewater chemicals are a set of compounds found in water affected by anthropogenic activities. Analytical results from nutrient, isotope, and wastewater chemical samples are available in U.S. Geological Survey (2010).

Nutrients

Concentrations of nitrogen species were analyzed in surface-water and groundwater samples collected in 2007–08. Results indicated that nitrate was the dominant species of dissolved nitrogen present in all samples (tables 3 and 4). Nitrate was the only bioavailable species detected at concentrations greater than the LRL in all surface-water samples. Average concentrations of dissolved nitrate in surface water were largest in samples collected from the two sites near Teton Village, A-R1U and A-R1D (table 5; fig. 8), and decreased downstream as far as site A-Wck. The average dissolved nitrate concentrations were greater at sites A-R6D and A-R7 than at site A-Wck. Average dissolved nitrate concentrations from the five downstream sites were similar to average concentrations of samples collected from streams and rivers in the Jackson Hole valley (table 5; Clark and others, 2007).

Two samples were collected for quality assurance of nutrient samples: one replicate sample and one blank sample. The relative-percent difference (RPD) between concentrations in the replicate sample was calculated to compare the concentrations measured in both the replicate and environmental samples using the following equation:

$$RPD = \text{absolute value}\left(\frac{sample1 - sample2}{\dfrac{sample1 + sample2}{2}}\right) \times 100$$

The RPD of all nutrients in the replicate ranged from 0 to 17 percent. The higher RPD is attributable to the small concentrations (0.13 and 0.11) in the samples.

The blank sample collected was used to evaluate potential introduction of contamination to environmental samples during field sample collection, field equipment cleaning, and laboratory analytical procedures. Water certified to be free of all inorganic chemicals, was used as the source water for all blank samples. Phosphorus was the only nutrient detected in the blank sample and was at an estimated concentration of 0.005 milligram per liter (mg/L), which is below the LRL of 0.008 mg/L.

Concentrations of dissolved nitrate at the two upstream sites (A-R1U and A-R1D) on Fish Creek with seasonal flow were always greater than concentrations at the five downstream sites with perennial flow (fig. 9A). The largest dissolved nitrate concentration of 0.32 mg/L was in the August 2007 sample from site A-R1U.

Average concentrations of dissolved nitrate in groundwater were higher in samples from two sites, A-R1D-W1 and A-Wck-W1, than in samples from the west bank area wells reported by Nolan and Miller (1995), whereas the average dissolved nitrate concentration at site A-R3D-W1 was lower than the average for the west bank area wells (table 5). Median nitrate concentrations in samples from wells completed in the geologic units to the west of Fish Creek (fig. 3), which may recharge the groundwater in the Fish Creek alluvium, ranged from 0.06 mg/L as nitrogen (N) for the Cambrian- and Precambrian-age units to 0.16 mg/L as N for the Mississippian- to Permian-age Tensleep Sandstone (Nolan and Miller, 1995). Geologic units potentially contributing groundwater to the western side of the Fish Creek alluvium are primarily Cambrian- and Precambrian-age units for the upper one-third of the Fish Creek drainage basin, with the addition of Mississippian to Permian-age formations and glacial units in the lower two-thirds of the basin. Dissolved nitrate concentrations in the groundwater were largest at all three sites in May compared to the other months sampled (fig. 9B; table 4).

Concentrations of dissolved nitrate in groundwater were consistently greater than concentrations in the corresponding surface-water samples during the same sampling events (tables 3 and 4; fig. 9B). As mentioned previously, the wells were designed to be in the flow path upstream from the corresponding surface-water site. The groundwater/surface-water pair with the most similar dissolved nitrate concentrations was sites A-R1D and A-R1D-W1. The consistent similarity is likely due to both the large groundwater recharge to the stream in this part of Fish Creek and that groundwater is a larger component of the streamflow compared to downstream. Groundwater samples from sites A-R3D-W1 and A-Wck-W1, in the upstream flow path of surface-water sites A-R3D and

Table 3. Physical properties, nutrient concentrations, and nitrate isotope values for surface-water samples from Fish Creek, Wyoming, 2007–08.

[°C, degrees C; m³/s, meter cubed per second; mg/L, milligrams per liter; µS/cm, microsiemens per centimeter at 25°C; E, estimated; <, less than; --, no data]

Site number	Date	Time	Air temper-ature (°C)	Instan-taneous streamflow (m³/s)	Dissolved oxygen (mg/L)	pH, unfiltered, (standard unit)	Specific conductance, unfiltered (µS/cm)	Water temper-ature (°C)	Ammonia, dissolved (mg/L as N)	Nitrate plus nitrite, dissolved (mg/L as N)
A-R1U	05/10/2007	1330	26.0	E0.06	8.6	8.2	73	13.0	<0.020	0.19
	07/10/2007	1300	--	.04	8.7	7.5	254	12 5	--	--
	08/13/2007	1430	32.0	.04	9 2	7.0	258	13.0	<.020	.32
A-R1D	07/10/2007	1730	--	.52	8.8	7.8	270	12.0	--	--
	08/16/2007	2045	--	1.27	5 1	7.5	268	13.0	<.020	.14
	08/18/2008	1730	--	.74	--	E8.2	265	--	<.020	.253
	10/23/2008	1330	E5.0	.06	10.8	8.2	243	11 3	<.020	.268
A-RB	03/09/2007	0900	2.0	E.01	16 3	8.5	223	4.0	<.020	.042
	05/08/2007	1700	--	.55	9.0	8.3	243	14.0	<.020	.115
	07/11/2007	1100	--	3.23	8 9	7.8	245	12 5	--	--
	08/15/2007	1600	25.0	3.14	9.4	7.9	221	16 5	<.020	.017
	10/22/2007	1700	--	.50	8 9	8.6	237	10.0	--	--
	05/06/2008	1500	20.5	.55	14.4	7.8	232	14 3	<.020	.154
	08/19/2008	1200	32.0	3.62	8.8	8.2	236	15.7	--	--
	10/20/2008	1620	4.0	1.13	8.8	8.2	221	11 1	<.020	.079
A-R3D	03/07/2007	1345	4.0	1.04	10.7	8.6	266	11.0	<.020	.04
	05/09/2007	0845	15.0	5.81	10.4	8.4	212	8 5	<.020	.034
	07/11/2007	1600	--	10.3	9.7	8.5	222	17.0	--	--
	08/14/2007	1515	--	9.54	8.0	8.4	203	17.0	<.020	<.016
	10/25/2007	0930	--	3.06	10.6	8.4	213	5.8	--	--
	05/06/2008	1730	15.0	1.92	8.8	8.6	250	11 1	<.020	.026
	08/19/2008	1630	28.0	9.23	8 3	8.3	220	15 2	<.020	.021
	10/21/2008	0830	-5.0	3.68	8.7	7.8	236	6.8	--	--
A-Wck	03/06/2007	1535	11.0	.85	11 1	8.9	282	11.0	<.020	.02
	05/08/2007	1040	22.5	4.81	11 1	8.7	220	9.0	E.014	.02
	07/12/2007	1000	--	11	8.8	8.0	226	12.0	--	--
	08/15/2007	1045	21.0	10.5	10.4	8.6	229	13 5	<.020	<.016
	10/24/2007	1700	--	3.0	11 2	9.1	230	9 5	--	--
	05/07/2008	1345	14.5	2.04	16.8	8.7	264	8 9	<.020	.024
	08/20/2008	0845	28.0	9.26	9 2	7.9	218	11.0	<.020	E.009
	10/22/2008	1630	E-2.0	4.45	10.6	9.4	224	9.0	<.020	<.016
A-R6D	03/07/2007	0910	-3.0	1.54	10 5	8.3	279	4.0	<.020	.084
	05/07/2007	0915	11.0	6.06	10 5	--	225	7.0	<.020	.05
	07/12/2007	1700	--	10.9	10 3	8.9	223	16 5	--	--
	08/16/2007	1230	26.0	10.7	10 3	8.8	230	15 5	<.020	<.016
	10/25/2007	1700	--	3.46	10.6	8.9	239	10.0	--	--
	05/08/2008	1045	9.0	3.43	15.7	8.7	272	8 1	<.020	.099
	08/20/2008	1500	19.0	9.46	11 3	9.2	225	15 5	<.020	<.016
	10/22/2008	1400	1.0	4.5	14 1	9.1	227	7.6	<.020	E.011
A-R7	05/08/2008	1645	14.0	4.25	9 2	8.7	271	10.9	<.020	.051
	08/21/2008	0845	17.0	10.4	9 2	8.1	245	10.8	<.020	<.016
	10/22/2008	0900	−1.0	5.72	9 5	8.0	254	4.5	<.020	E.008

Table 3. Physical properties, nutrient concentrations, and nitrate isotope values for surface-water samples from Fish Creek, Wyoming, 2007–08.—Continued

[°C, degrees C; m³/s, meter cubed per second; mg/L, milligrams per liter; μS/cm, microsiemens per centimeter at 25°C; E, estimated; <, less than; --, no data]

Site number	Date	Nitrate, dissolved (mg/L as N)	Nitrite, dissolved (mg/L as N)	Total nitrogen,[1] dissolved (mg/L as N)	Total nitrogen,[1] unfiltered (mg/L as N)	Ortho-phosphate, dissolved (mg/L as P)	Total phosphorus, dissolved (mg/L as P)	Total phosphorus, unfiltered (mg/L as P)	N-15/N-14 ratio in nitrate (per mil)	O-18/O-16 ratio in nitrate (per mil)
A-R1U	05/10/2007	0.19	<0.002	0.30	0.70	0.016	0.014	0.19	2.35	−4.40
	07/10/2007	--	--	--	--	--	--	--	--	--
	08/13/2007	.32	<.002	.39	.33	.012	.01	.024	5.84	−7.11
A-R1D	07/10/2007	--	--	--	--	--	--	--	--	--
	08/16/2007	.14	<.002	.34	.17	.035	.033	.044	9.77	−5.12
	08/18/2008	.253	<.002	.47	.27	.047	.048	.050	--	--
	10/23/2008	E.27	E.001	.37	.28	.065	.065	.067	--	--
A-RB	03/09/2007	.042	<.002	.08	.11	E.005	E.003	E.005	4.70	−5.52
	05/08/2007	.115	<.002	.16	.20	E.006	E.004	.009	4.89	−7.36
	07/11/2007	--	--	--	--	--	--	--	--	--
	08/15/2007	.017	<.002	.07	.08	.012	.015	.021	7.12	−5.59
	10/22/2007	--	--	--	--	--	--	--	--	--
	05/06/2008	E.15	E.001	.42	.27	.007	E.005	.011	--	--
	08/19/2008		--	--	.15	--	--	.020	--	--
	10/20/2008	E.08	E.002	.22	.12	.009	.009	.012	--	--
A-R3D	03/07/2007	.04	<.002	.11	.15	.008	.009	.011	6.17	−4.94
	05/09/2007	E.03	E.002	.09	.13	E.004	E.003	.013	5.60	−4.69
	07/11/2007	--	--	--	--	--	--	--	--	--
	08/14/2007	<.016	<.002	.17	.09	.008	.009	.017	--	--
	10/25/2007	--	--	--	--	--	--	--	--	--
	05/06/2008	.026	<.002	.19	.15	E.005	<.006	.010	--	--
	08/19/2008	.021	<.002	.29	.12	E.003	.007	.013	--	--
	10/21/2008	--	--	--	--	--	--	--	--	--
A-Wck	03/06/2007	E.02	E.001	.12	.12	E.006	.010	.012	--	--
	05/08/2007	E.02	E.002	.07	.12	E.004	E.003	.008	--	--
	07/12/2007	--	--	--	--	--	--	--	--	--
	08/15/2007	<.016	<.002	.28	.07	.007	.009	.014	--	--
	10/24/2007	--	--	--	--	--	--	--	--	--
	05/07/2008	E.02	E.002	.14	.10	E.005	<.006	E.005	--	--
	08/20/2008	E.01	E.001	.2	.10	E.005	E.006	.012	--	--
	10/22/2008	<.016	<.002	E.10	E.07	E.006	E.004	E.006	--	--
A-R6D	03/07/2007	E.08	E.001	.21	.16	E.005	.007	.011	6.40	−5.18
	05/07/2007	.05	.004	.10	.14	E.004	.008	.015	8.72	−2.63
	07/12/2007	--	--	--	--	--	--	--	--	--
	08/16/2007	<.016	<.002	.07	.07	.007	.009	.013	--	--
	10/25/2007	--	--	--	--	--	--	--	--	--
	05/08/2008	E.10	E.002	.27	.19	E.006	<.006	.013	--	--
	08/20/2008	<.016	<.002	.26	.16	.007	E.005	.011	--	--
	10/22/2008	E.011	<.002	.15	E.06	E.007	E.004	E.005	--	--
A-R7	05/08/2008	E.05	E.001	.27	.14	.006	E.004	.008	--	--
	08/21/2008	<.016	<.002	.09	E.06	.006	E.004	E.007	--	--
	10/22/2008	E.008	<.002	.14	E.06	E.006	E.003	<.008	--	--

[1]nitrate + nitrite + ammonia + organic nitrogen.

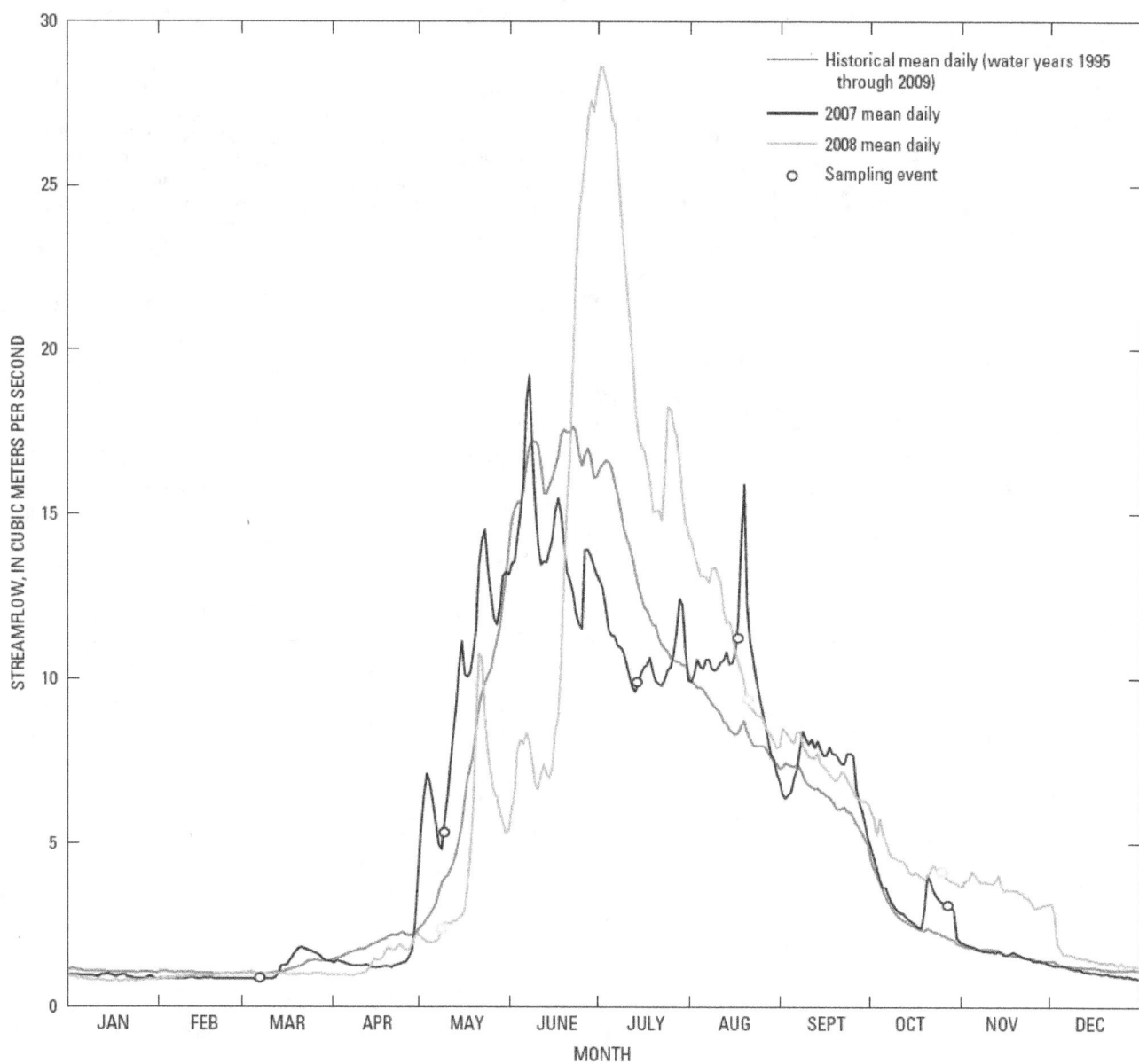

Figure 4. Historical mean daily streamflow and mean daily streamflow for 2007 and 2008 at streamflow-gaging station 13016450, Fish Creek at Wilson, Wyoming.

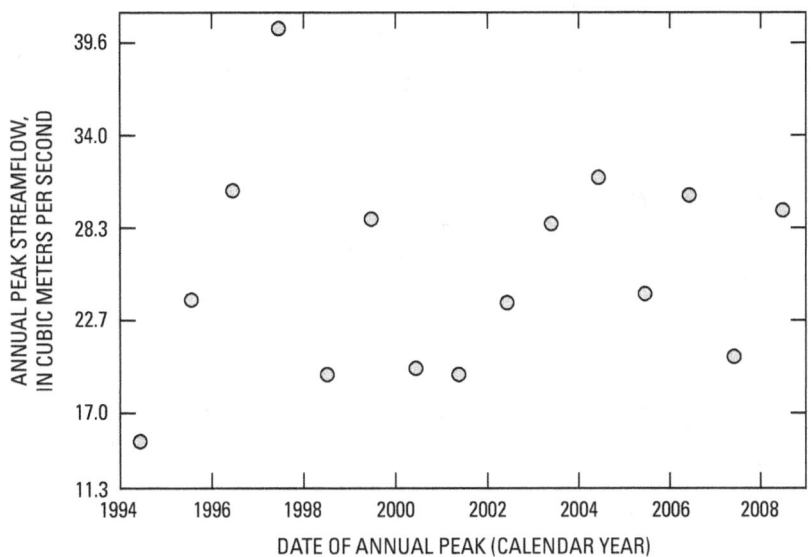

Figure 5.   Annual peak streamflow at streamflow-gaging station 13016450,
Fish Creek at Wilson, Wyoming,1994–2008.

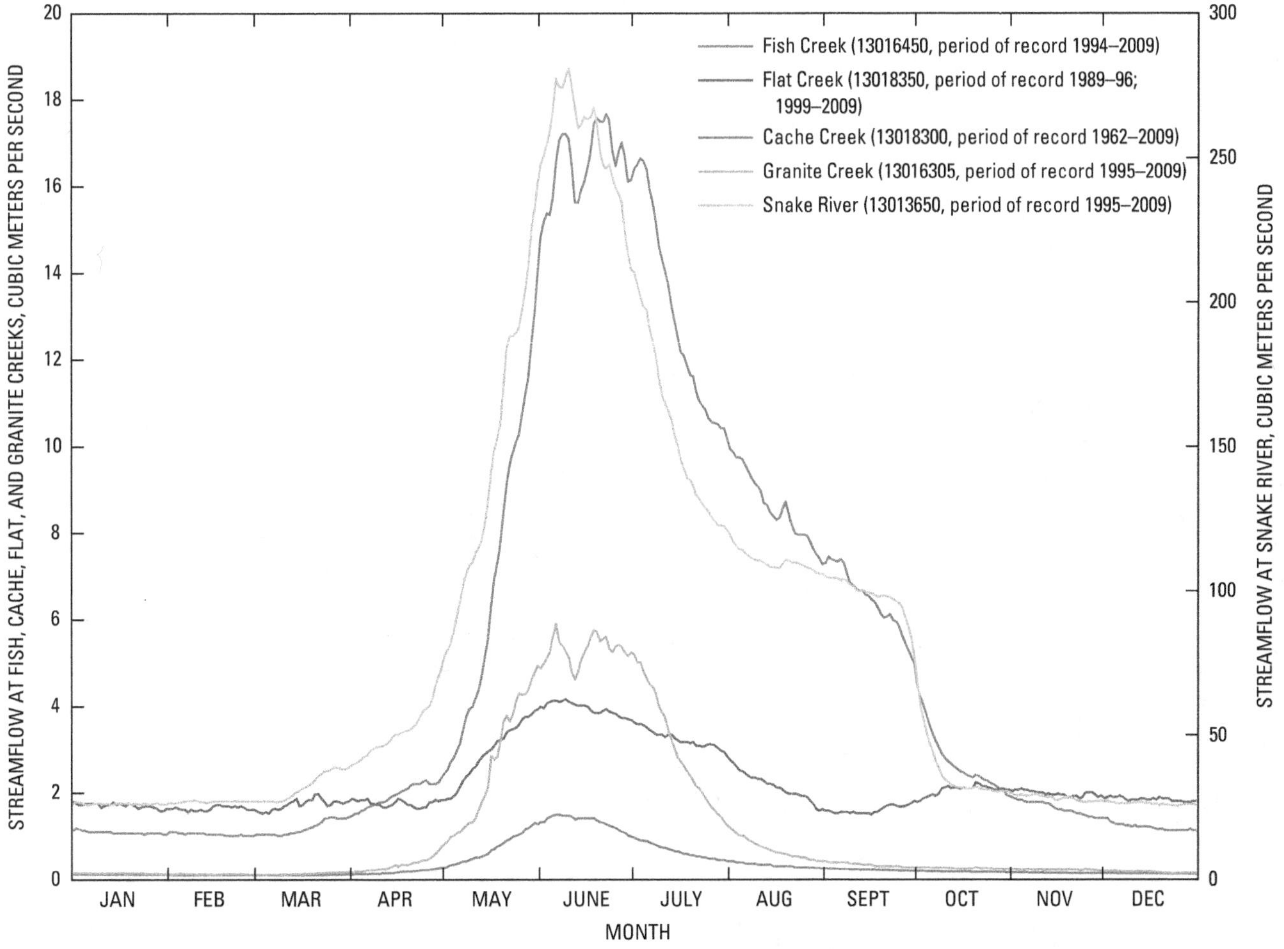

Figure 6.   Average mean daily streamflow at streamflow-gaging stations in Jackson Hole, Wyoming.

Table 4. Physical properties, nutrient concentrations, and nitrate isotope values for groundwater samples from wells near Fish Creek, Wyoming, 2007–08.

[C, degrees C; m, meter; mg/L, milligrams per liter; µS/cm, microsiemens per centimeter; NGVD 29, National Geodetic Vertical Datum of 1929; E, estimated; <, less than; --, no data]

Site number	Date	Time	Air temperature (°C)	Depth to water below land surface (m)	Dissolved oxygen (mg/L)	pH, unfiltered (standard unit)	Specific conductance unfiltered (µS/cm)	Water temperature (°C)	Altitude of land surface (meters above NGVD 29)	Ammonia, dissolved (mg/L as N)	Nitrate plus nitrite, dissolved (mg/L as N)
A-R1D-W1	05/10/2007	1145	--	1.38	7.7	7.2	273	7.0	2,184	<0.020	0.718
	08/16/2007	1915	--	.23	3.9	7.2	266	13.7	2,184	<.020	.328
	05/04/2008	1615	14	1.58	10	7.2	257	3.8	2,184	<.020	1.10
	08/21/2008	1810	--	.26	3.0	6.9	265	13.9	2,184	<.020	.336
	10/23/2008	1210	E5.0	.75	3.4	6.9	205	10.9	2,184	<.020	.321
A-R3D-W1	03/08/2007	1830	5	1.01	3.0	7.6	279	3.0	2,151	0.029	.269
	05/09/2007	1230	21	.70	2.7	7.1	301	7.5	2,151	<.020	.415
	08/13/2007	1245	29.5	.64	2.1	6.5	292	12.5	2,151	<.020	.105
	05/07/2008	1615	15	.87	4.6	7.4	292	5.1	2,151	<.020	.296
	08/21/2008	1330	17	.72	1.7	7.1	302	11.7	2,151	<.020	.109
	10/23/2008	1150	E5.0	.83	2.4	7.2	256	8.0	2,151	<.020	.127
A-Wck-W1	03/08/2007	1600	--	.94	2.0	7.6	318	4.5	2,140	<.020	.456
	05/08/2007	1245	22.5	.74	1.6	7.3	305	7.6	2,140	E.011	.725
	08/16/2007	1530	--	.58	1.4	7.3	300	13.5	2,140	<.020	.215
	05/07/2008	1430	14.5	.88	4.0	7.3	329	6.0	2,140	<.020	1.42
	08/21/2008	1500	17	.63	.8	7.1	313	12.8	2,140	<.020	.227
	10/23/2008	1100	E5.0	.48	1.3	7.3	254	10.6	2,140	<.020	.357

Table 4. Physical properties, nutrient concentrations, and nitrate isotope values for groundwater samples from wells near Fish Creek, Wyoming, 2007–08.—Continued

[C, degrees C; m, meter; mg/L, milligrams per liter; µS/cm, microsiemens per centimeter; NGVD 29, National Geodetic Vertical Datum of 1929; E, estimated; <, less than; --, no data]

Site number	Date	Nitrate, dissolved (mg/L as N)	Nitrite, dissolved (mg/L as N)	Orthophosphate, dissolved (mg/L as P)	Total phosphorus, dissolved (mg/L as P)	Total phosphorus, unfiltered (mg/L as P)	Total nitrogen,[1] dissolved (mg/L as N)	Total nitrogen,[1] unfiltered (mg/L as N)	N-15/N-14 ratio in nitrate (per mil)	O-18/O-16 ratio in nitrate (per mil)
A-R1D-W1	05/10/2007	0.718	<.002	0.051	0.060	0.123	0.87	0.85	8.38	-6.96
	08/16/2007	.328	<.002	.057	.062	.069	.50	.34	7.81	-9.36
	05/04/2008	1.10	<.002	.036	.041	.046	1.27	1.17	--	--
	08/21/2008	.336	<.002	.055	.055	.105	.47	.41	--	--
	10/23/2008	.321	<.002	.044	.044	.046	.43	.32	--	--
A-R3D-W1	03/08/2007	.267	E.002	.020	.041	.207	.77	.74	6.89	-7.49
	05/09/2007	.415	<.002	.012	.010	.011	.53	.48	10.03	-5.09
	08/13/2007	.105	<.002	.017	.013	.024	.16	.13	6.31	-5.22
	05/07/2008	.296	<.002	.018	.013	.038	.40	.39	--	--
	08/21/2008	.109	<.002	.016	.013	.012	.27	.16	--	--
	10/23/2008	.127	<.002	.014	.011	.011	.22	.12	--	--
A-Wck-W1	03/08/2007	.456	<.002	.036	.039	.045	.47	.47	8.05	-8.00
	05/08/2007	.725	<.002	.047	.048	.049	.84	.79	7.35	-6.18
	08/16/2007	.215	<.002	.049	.055	.056	.43	.24	10.54	-6.87
	05/07/2008	1.42	<.002	.052	.048	.050	1.54	1.53	--	--
	08/21/2008	.227	<.002	.045	.044	.043	.28	.24	--	--
	10/23/2008	.357	<.002	.060	.047	.046	.49	.37	--	--

[1]nitrate + nitrite + ammonia + organic nitrogen.

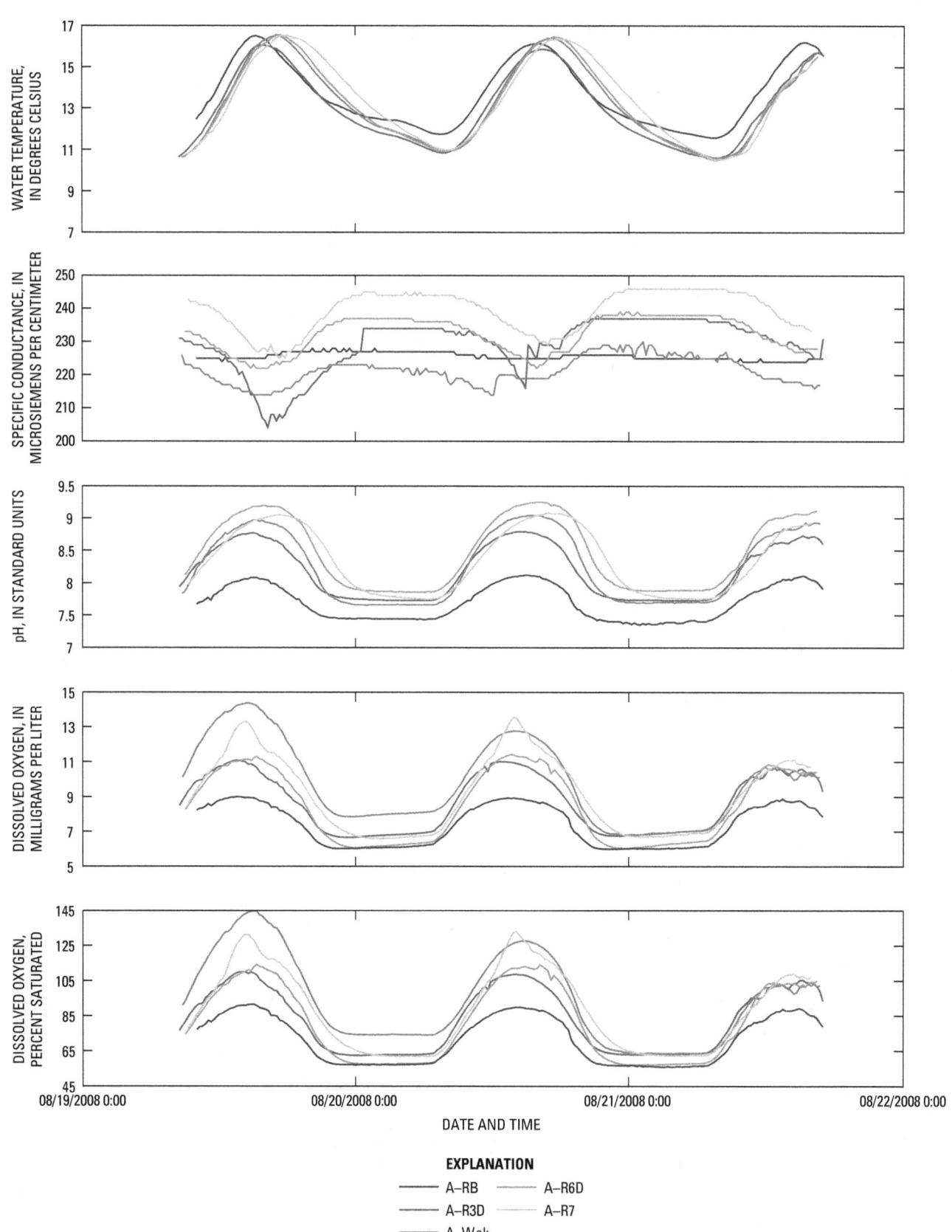

Figure 7.   Continuously collected measurements of water-quality properties from surface-water sites on Fish Creek, Wyoming, August 2008.

Table 5. Average concentrations of dissolved nitrate and orthophosphate in samples from Fish Creek (2007–08), Jackson Hole streams and rivers, and area groundwater.

[mg/L, milligram per liter; N, nitrogen; P, phosphorus; <, less than]

Site name (number)	Nitrate		Orthophosphate	
	Number of samples	Average concentration (mg/L as N)	Number of samples	Average concentration (mg/L as P)
Surface-water samples from Fish Creek (2007–08)				
A-R1U (433505110494001)	2	0.26	2	0.01
A-R1D (433438110495901)	3	.22	3	.05
A-RB (433302110504701)	5	.08	5	.01
A-R3D (433117110515101)	5	.02	5	.01
A-Wck (13016450)	6	.01	6	.01
A-R6D (432906110522601)	6	.04	6	.01
A-R7 (432748110515301)	3	.04	3	.01
Jackson Hole valley streams and rivers (2006)				
Snake River at Moose (13013650)	87	0.02	84	0.01
Cache Creek (13018300)	118	.13	97	.02
Granite Creek (433655110494101 and 13016305)[1]	8	.05	8	.001
Lake Creek (433908110482201 and 433738110465301)[1]	8	.04	8	.001
Cottonwood Creek (13012800 and 13013000)[1]	7	.02	7	<.006
Taggert Creek (434222110454601 and 13012900)[1]	8	.11	8	<.006
Groundwater samples from Fish Creek area (2007–08)				
A-R1D-W1 (433431110501101)	5	0.96	5	0.05
A-R3D-W1 (433122110514201)	6	.21	6	.02
A-Wck-W1 (433005110521801)	6	.58	6	.05
Groundwater samples in Teton County (1991–93)				
West bank area wells[2]	14	0.36	14	0.01

[1]Average concentrations are calculated from samples collected at two sites on the creek in 2006 as described in Clark and others (2007).

[2]Average concentrations are calculated from samples collected during July 1991, 1992, and 1993 as part of the evallation of resources in Teton County (Nolan and Miller, 1995).

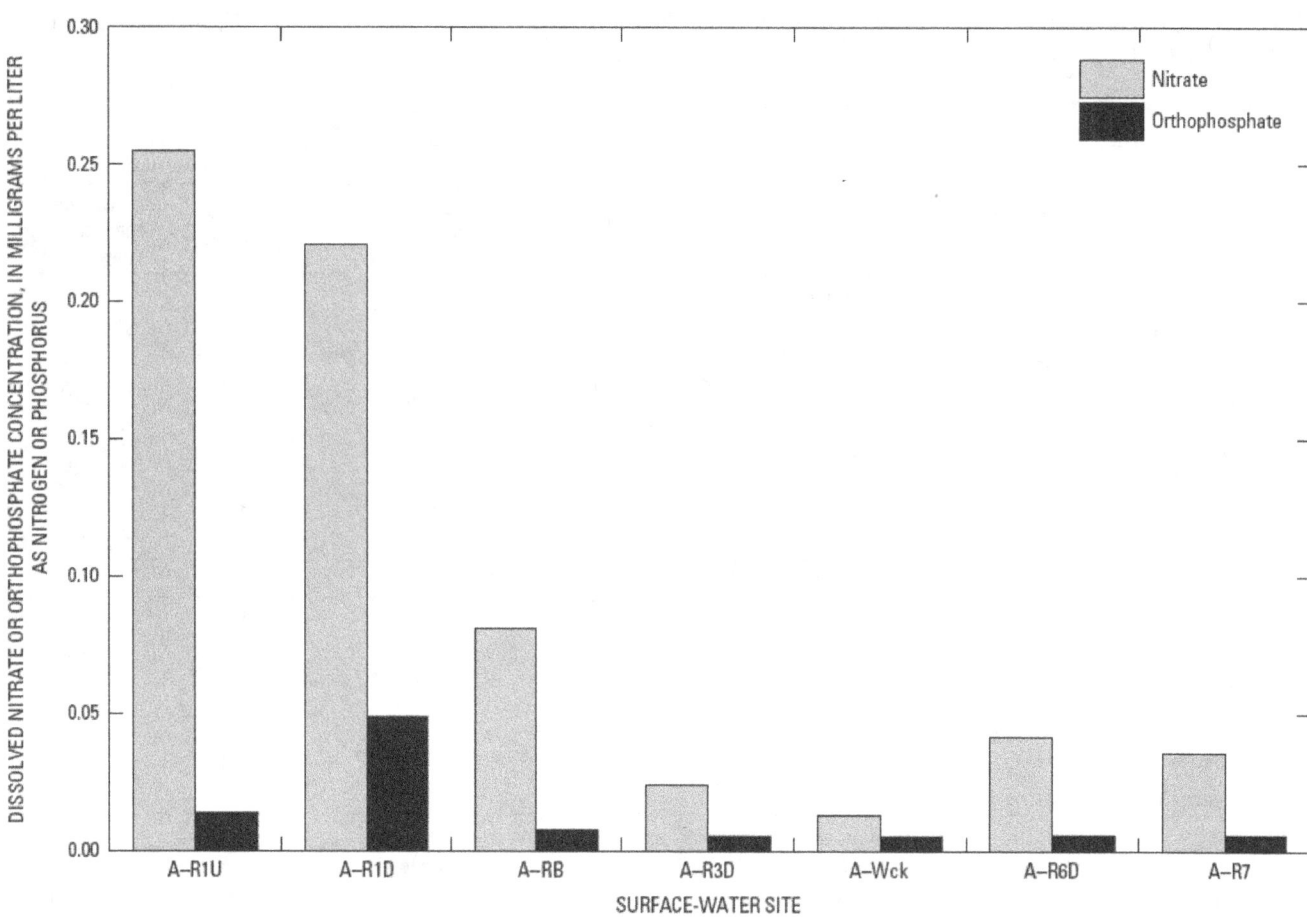

Figure 8.   Average concentrations of dissolved nitrate and orthophosphate in samples from surface-water sites, Fish Creek, Wyoming, 2007–08.

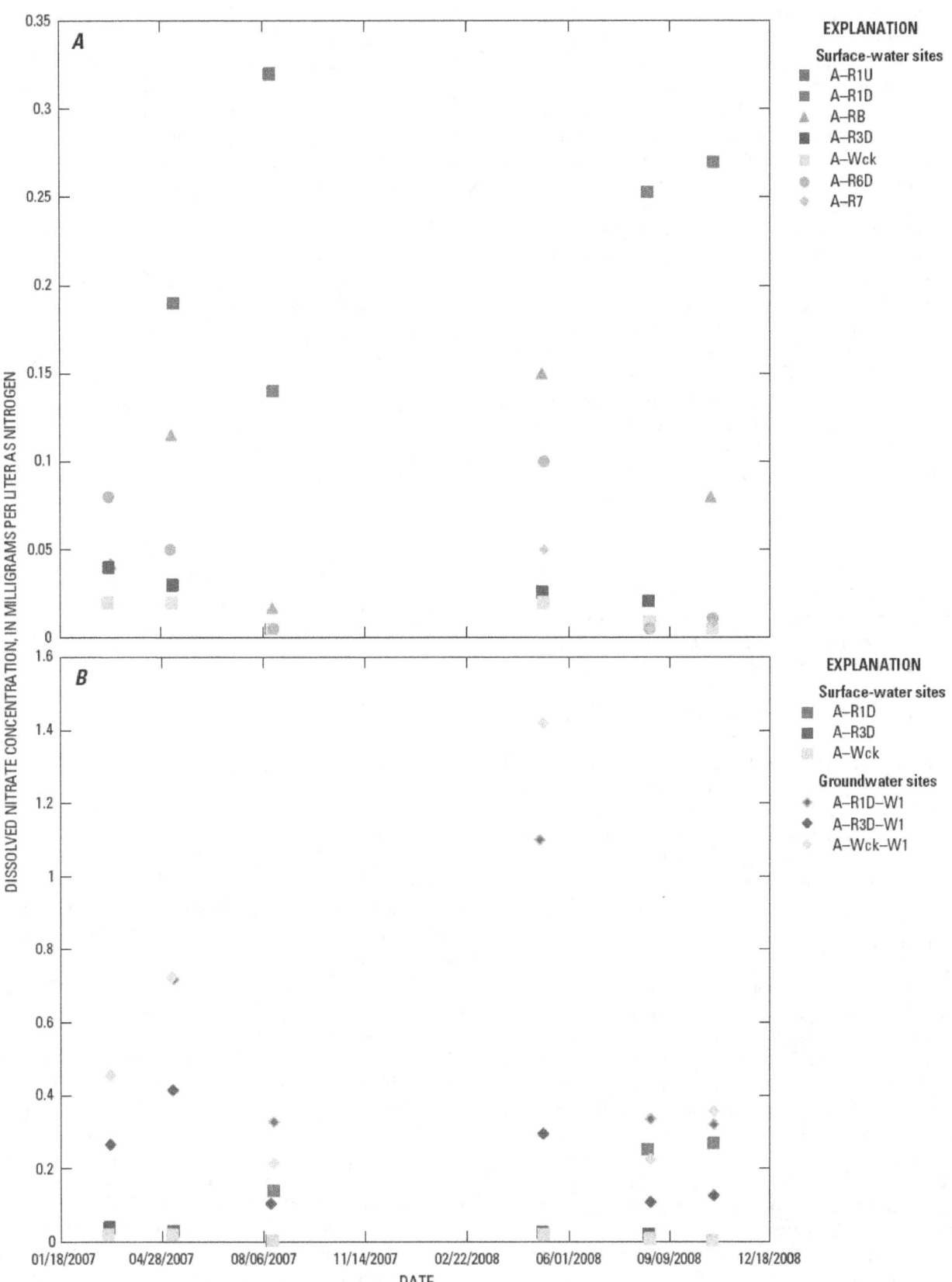

Figure 9. Dissolved nitrate concentrations. *A*, Surface-water samples and *B*, groundwater and selected surface-water samples, Fish Creek area, Wyoming, 2007–08.

A-Wck, respectively, had dissolved nitrate concentrations at least 10 times greater than concentrations in the corresponding surface-water samples (fig. 9B).

Concentrations of phosphorus species were analyzed in surface-water and groundwater samples collected during 2007–08. Analytical results indicate that orthophosphate was the primary dissolved species of phosphorus present in all samples (tables 3 and 4). The average concentration of dissolved ortho-phosphate in surface-water samples was largest (0.05 mg/L as phosphorus [P]) in samples collected from the upstream site A-R1D near Teton Village (fig. 10A); samples from all other sites had an equal average concentration of 0.01 mg/L as P (table 5; fig. 8). Average dissolved orthophosphate concentra-tions for Fish Creek were similar to average concentrations in samples collected from two streams and rivers in the Jackson Hole valley (Snake River and Cache Creek) and were at least 10 times greater than concentrations in samples from four other streams in the valley (Granite, Lake, Cottonwood, and Taggert Creeks; table 5) reported by Clark and others (2007).

Average concentrations of dissolved orthophosphate in the groundwater were higher in samples from all three sites, A-R1D-W1, A-R3D-W1, and A-Wck-W1, than in samples from the west bank area wells (table 5). Median dissolved orthophosphate concentrations in samples from wells com-pleted in the geologic units to the west of Fish Creek (fig. 3), which may recharge the groundwater in the Fish Creek alluvium, ranged from less than (<) 0.010 mg/L as P for the Cambrian- and Precambrian-age units to 0.08 mg/L as P for the Tensleep Sandstone (Nolan and Miller, 1995).

Concentrations of dissolved orthophosphate in ground-water typically were greater than concentrations in the corre-sponding surface-water sites during the same sampling events (tables 3 and 4; fig. 10B). The groundwater/surface-water pair with the most similar dissolved orthophosphate concentrations were sites A-R1D and A-R1D-W1. The consistent similarity likely is due to the large groundwater recharge to the stream in the upstream part of Fish Creek.

Isotopes of Nitrate

A nitrate molecule is composed of one nitrogen atom and three oxygen atoms. Isotopes of a particular element have the same number of protons in the atomic nucleus but differ-ent numbers of neutrons, resulting in different atomic masses (heavy or light isotopes). The relative abundance of the nitro-gen and oxygen isotopes in nitrate can be precisely measured using mass spectrometry. Many chemical and physical pro-cesses can produce large variations in the relative abundance of nitrogen and oxygen isotopes in nitrate. In general terms, the oxygen isotopic composition of nitrate indicates how the nitrate was formed, whereas the nitrogen isotopic composition can help discern the sources of the nitrate (Clark and Fritz, 1997; Kendall and McDonnell, 1998).

Stable isotopes of nitrate typically are reported using delta (δ), which compares the ratio between heavy and light isotopes of a sample to that of a reference standard. Delta

values are expressed as a difference in parts per thousand or per mil, from values of a reference standard. In this report, $\delta^{15}N$ ($^{15}N/^{14}N$) values are reported in per mil relative to atmo-spheric nitrogen (AIR), and $\delta^{18}O$ ($^{18}O/^{16}O$) values are reported in per mil relative to Vienna Standard Mean Ocean Water (VSMOW). The value for δ is calculated using the following equation (Clark and Fritz, 1997):

$$\delta \text{ (in per mil)} = [(Rx/Rs) - 1] \times 1{,}000 \tag{1}$$

where:
Rx is the ratio of the heavy-to-light isotope of the sample, and
Rs is the ratio of the heavy-to-light isotope of the applicable reference standard (AIR or VSMOW).

Eighteen samples were collected from Fish Creek and nearby groundwater for analyses of nitrogen and oxygen isotopes of nitrate (NO_3). One replicate samples was also collected and analyzed, and the RPD was 0.3 percent for $\delta^{15}N$ [NO_3] and 26 percent for $\delta^{18}O$ [NO_3]. The $\delta^{18}O$ [NO_3] values from samples collected from Fish Creek and nearby groundwater (fig. 11) ranged from about –2.6 to –9.4. The $\delta^{15}N$ [NO_3] values ranged from about 2.4 to 10.5.

During March and May of 2007, $\delta^{15}N$ [NO_3] values and nitrate concentrations from groundwater samples generally were higher than values from surface-water samples (figs. 11 and 12). Also noted during March and May is an increase in the $\delta^{15}N$ [NO_3] values in the downstream direction. During August 2007, the $\delta^{15}N$ [NO_3] values and nitrate concentrations had similar distributions.

Wastewater Chemicals

Sixty-one wastewater chemicals were analyzed in samples collected from Fish Creek and nearby groundwater in 2007 (table 19, in the "Supplemental Data" section). Additionally, samples of certified laboratory-grade, organic-free water were collected, processed, and analyzed as blank samples in the same manner for the same chemicals as the environmental samples.

Twenty-one different chemicals were detected in the samples from Fish Creek. The majority of the detections were at very low concentrations; most detections were near the LRL and many were qualified as a detection confirmed, but not quantified. Seven chemicals (camphor, N,N-diethyl-*meta*-toluamide (DEET), fluoranthene, isophorone, menthol, methyl salicylate, and phenanthrene) that were detected in at least one environmental sample had corresponding detections in blank samples; pyrene also was detected in a blank sample but not in any of the environmental samples. Because of the very low concentrations and the risk of contamination from many sources of these everyday chemicals, it can be difficult to inter-pret the results of chemical detections. During interpretation, it is helpful to note the number of detections in a sample, the groupings of types of chemicals, the concentrations of detec-tions, and the detections of the chemical in blank samples.

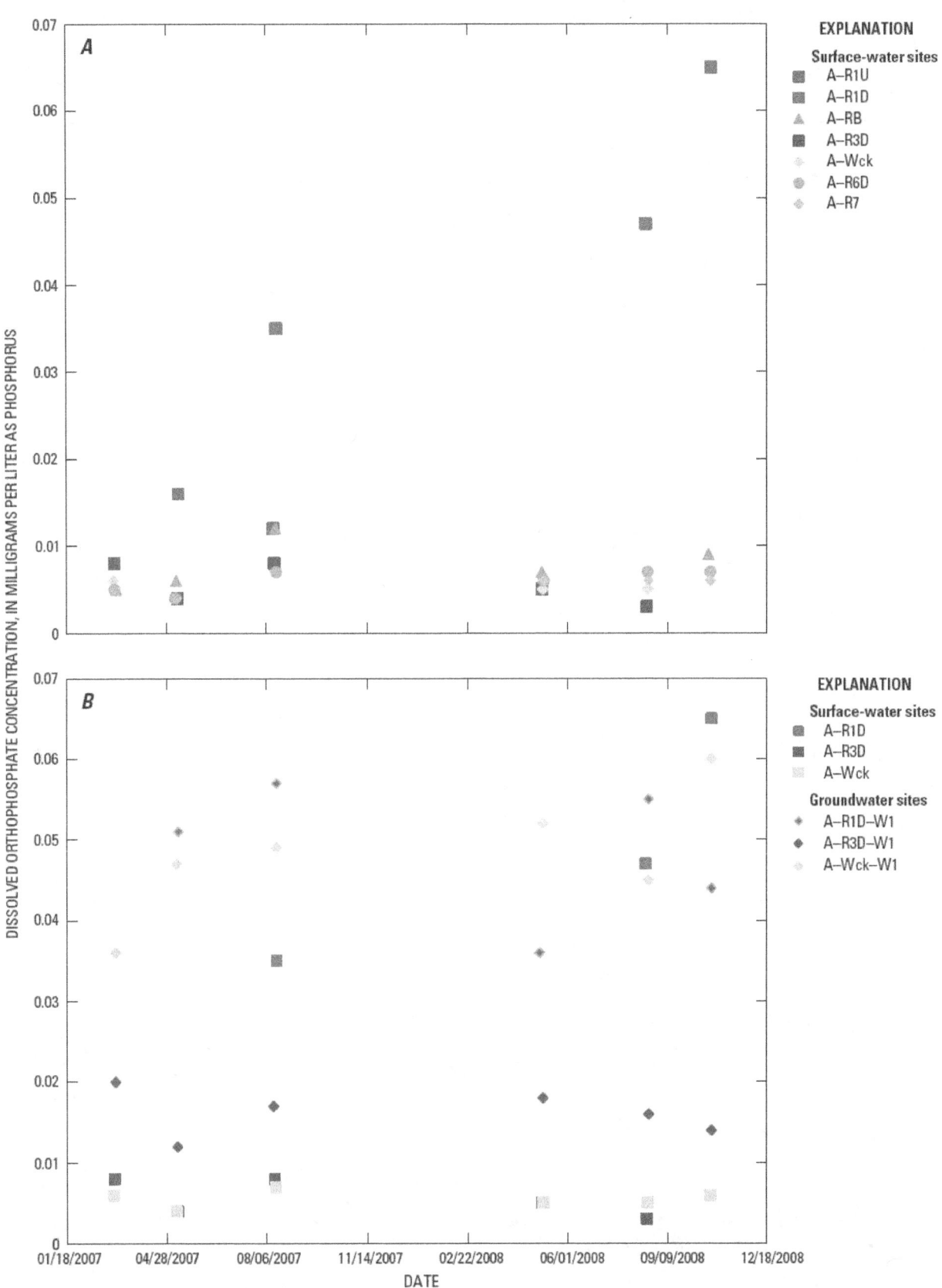

Figure 10. Dissolved orthophosphate concentrations. *A*, Surface-water samples, and *B*, groundwater and selected surface-water samples, Fish Creek area, Wyoming, 2007–08.

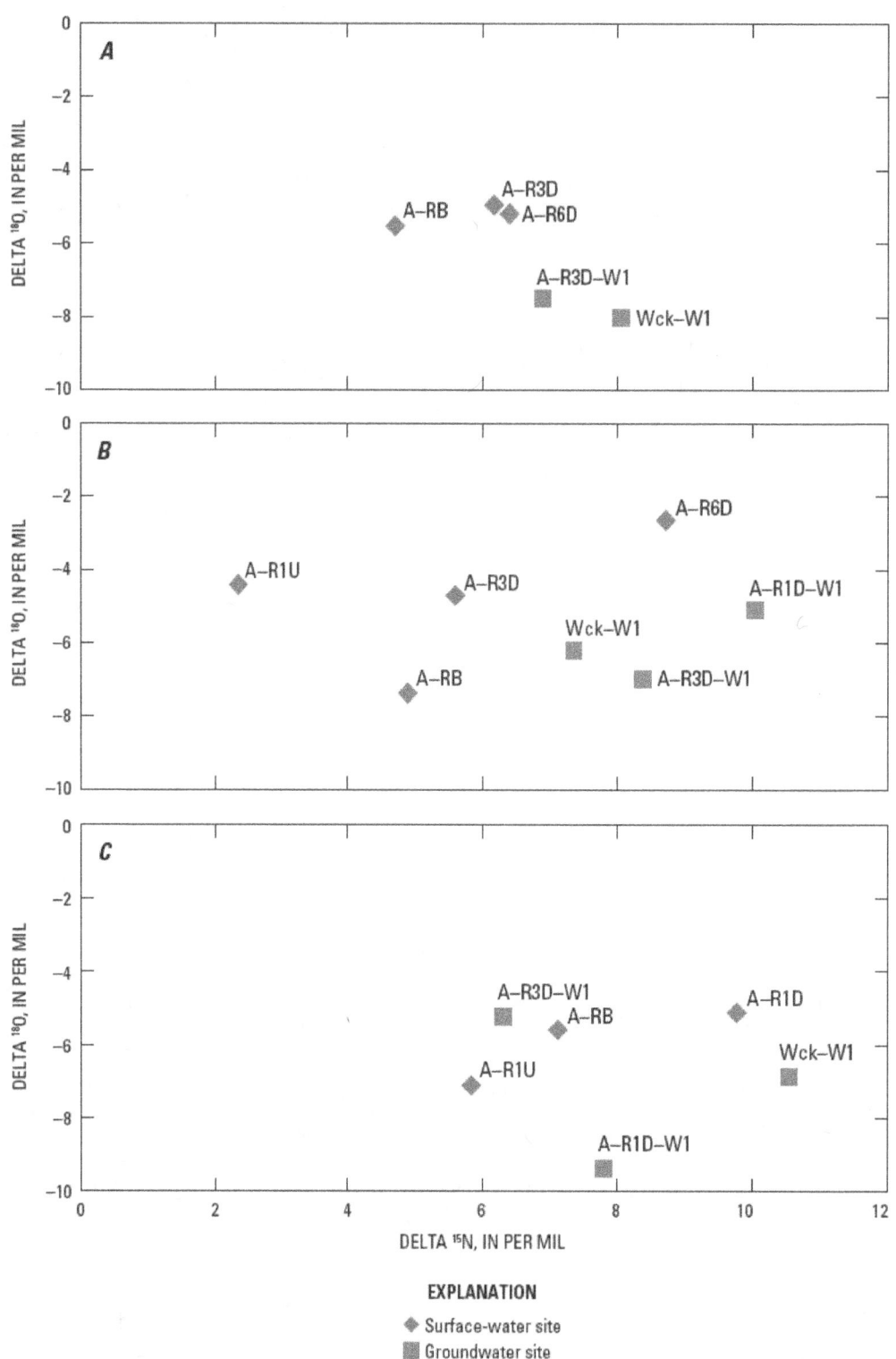

Figure 11. Isotopic composition of nitrate in samples collected from Fish Creek and nearby groundwater. *A*, March 2007; *B*, May 2007; and *C*, August 2007.

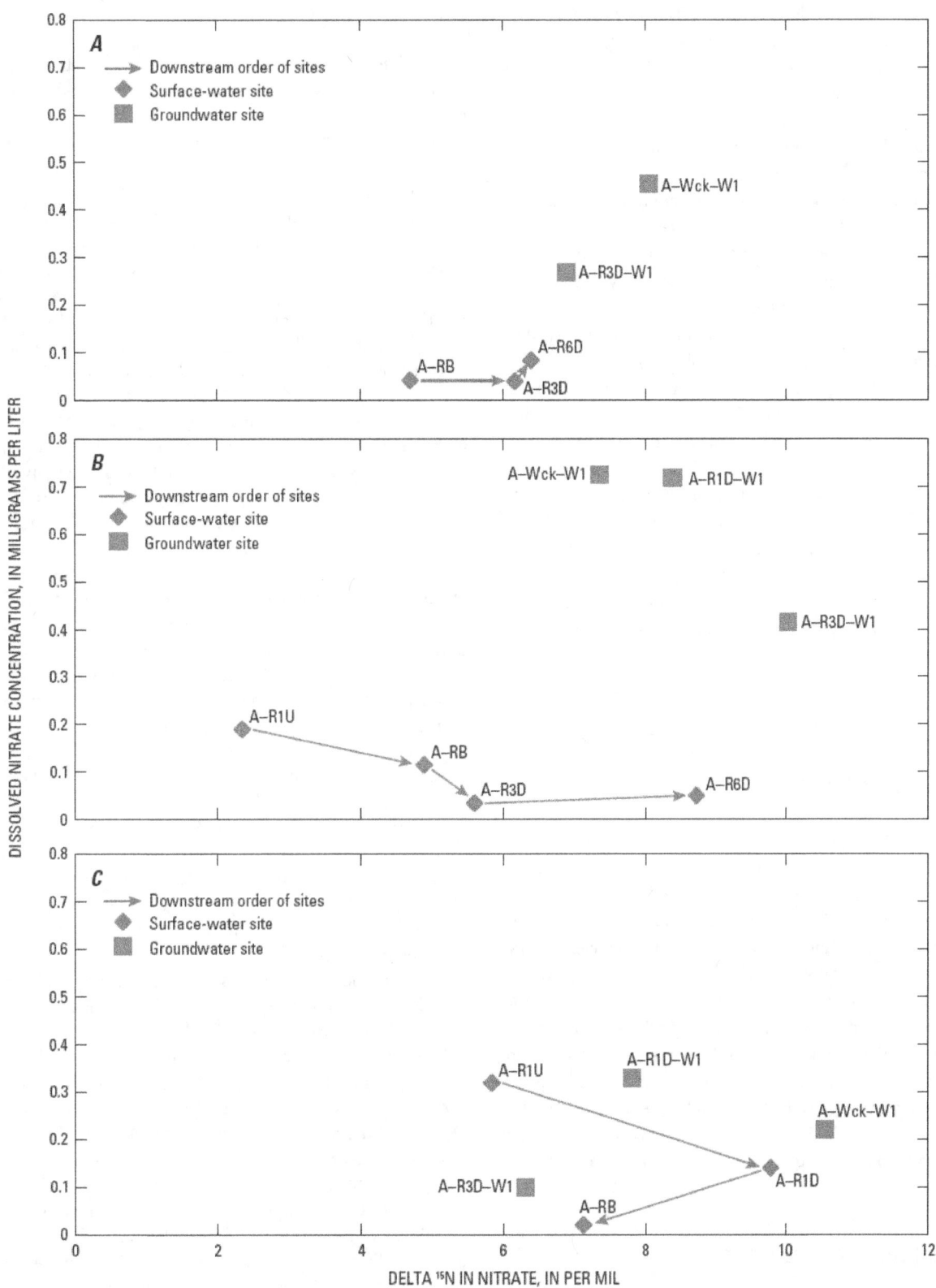

Figure 12. Dissolved nitrate concentrations and isotopic composition of nitrate in samples collected from Fish Creek and nearby groundwater. *A*, March 2007; *B*, May 2007; and *C*, August 2007.

Three samples had detections of wastewater chemicals that likely indicate anthropogenic activities affecting the water in and near Fish Creek. Two samples had detections of chemicals not detected in blank samples. A sample collected in August 2007 at site A-R1U had detections of four chemicals that likely would be found together from a similar water-use activity. The chemicals detected (caffeine, 3-methyl-1H-indole, *para*-nonylphenol, and tributyl phosphate) are all likely to be found in household items (included in the detected chemicals are flavors and disinfectants) (table 10 in "Supplemental Data"). The third sample likely to indicate anthropogenic activity affecting the water is the March 2007 sample from site A-R3D-W1. Although this sample only had two detected chemicals (*p*-cresol and phenol) that were not detected in blank samples, phenol (a disinfectant) was detected at a concentration of 1.4 micrograms per liter (µg/L), which was 1 µg/L greater than the LRL and was interpreted as an indication of an anthropogenic effect. Samples from several other sites had detections of wastewater chemicals; however, because of the very small concentrations, the small number of related compounds detected, and the possibility of contamination in either the field or laboratory of these common chemicals, these detections were not considered to indicate the presence of anthropogenic chemicals in the surface water or groundwater.

Biological Community and Habitat Characterization

Biological samples (aquatic plants and macroinvertebrates) were collected and habitat characteristics were measured at surface-water sites to characterize the biological communities of Fish Creek. For the aquatic plants, community composition, productivity, and algal communities were characterized. For the macroinvertebrate communities, composition and traits were characterized. For habitat characterizations, riparian canopy and streambed substrate (pebble counts) were measured. Algal and macroinvertebrate taxonomy data are presented in terms of community composition and traits because the algal and macroinvertebrate communities act as integrators of environmental variables such as water quality over a longer time period than a water-quality sample or measurement collected at one point in time.

Aquatic Plant Communities

When viewed from the shore or a bridge, Fish Creek commonly appeared to be bright green due to a green mat of aquatic plants on the bottom of the creek (fig. 13). The mat typically was composed of a mixture of macrophytes, macroalgae, microalgae, and moss.

Aquatic Plant Community Composition

The most common components of the aquatic plant community in Fish Creek were submergent macrophytes (large, rooted plants); macroalgae, classified as either *Cladophora* or other macroalgae; and microalgae (fig. 14). Samples of the visually dominant macrophytes were collected during a few sampling events for taxonomic identification. A narrow-leaved, grasslike macrophyte collected at site A-RB during May and August 2007 was identified as *Potamogeton filiformis*. Long-stemmed, leafy macrophytes collected from site A-R6D included *Myriophyllum* (probably *M. sibiricum*; water milfoil) in May and August 2007, and *Ranunculus aquatilis* (buttercup family) in August. The filamentous green alga *Cladophora* is shown as a macroalgae in figure 14 because of its abundance and habit of growing in long branched filaments (commonly 20–30 cm long), whereas the category of other macroalgae includes species such as *Nostoc*, a blue-green algae that grows in ball or ear-shaped colonies. Aquatic moss (Bryophyta) and areas of unsuitable substrate generally composed a relatively small proportion of the aquatic plant community composition.

The composition of the aquatic plant community in Fish Creek appeared to shift in the downstream direction in 2007. On average, the proportion of macrophytes ranged from about 1 percent at site A-R1U, the most upstream site, to 54 percent of the plant community at site A-R6D, the farthest downstream site sampled during 2007 (fig. 14). The downstream increase in macrophytes was accompanied by a downstream decrease in microalgae. The average proportion of microalgae ranged from 80 percent at site A-R1U to 24 percent at site A-R6D. The seasonal nature of the flow at sites A-R1U and A-R1D likely discourages the growth of longer-lived plants, such as macrophytes, moss, and *Cladophora,* that were observed in higher proportions at sites A-RB, A-R3, A-Wck, and A-R6D, which have perennial streamflow (fig. 14). The downstream pattern observed in 2007 was not repeated in 2008, perhaps due to environmental variables such as timing and volume of streamflow between years.

The proportion of the macroalgae *Cladophora* in the aquatic plant community was relatively high at sites A-Wck and A-R3D in both 2007 and 2008 (fig. 14). *Cladophora* at site A-Wck made up an average of about 40 percent of the plant community in 2007 and 46 percent in 2008. At site A-R3D, *Cladophora* made up an average of 30 percent in 2007 and 34 percent in 2008 of the plant community.

On a seasonal basis, the proportion of *Cladophora* was relatively stable at site A-Wck in 2007, accounting for about 40 percent of the plant observations during each of the five sampling events (fig. 15). In 2008, however, *Cladophora* was virtually absent from site A-Wck in May and made up 65–70 percent of the observations in August and October. This pattern was consistent at the other sites in 2008—*Cladophora* was absent from the May surveys and increased later in the summer. At site A-R3D, for example, *Cladophora* was not recorded in May but made up 82 percent of the observations in August 2008. The causes for the differences in the proportion

Site A–R1D, August 2007

Site A–RB, August 2007

Site A–R3D, August 2007

Site A–Wck, August 2007

Site A–R6D, August 2008

Site A–R7, August 2008

Figure 13.   Aquatic plant life in Fish Creek at sites A-R1D, A-RB, A-R3D, A-Wck, A-R6D, and A-R7, 2007 and 2008.

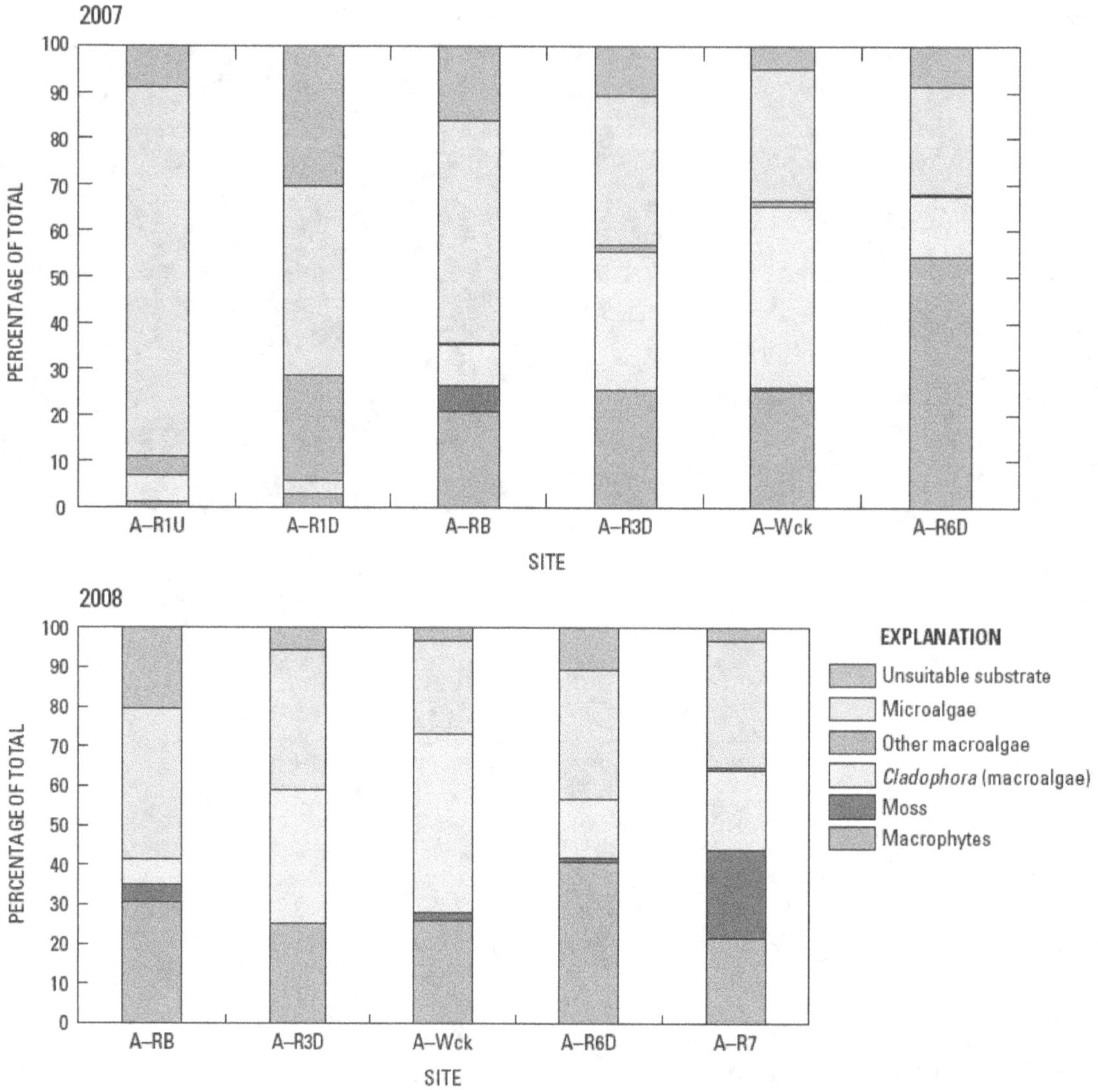
2007
100
90
80
70
60
50
40
30
20
10
0
PERCENTAGE OF TOTAL
A–R1U
A–R1D
A–RB
A–R3D
A–Wck
A–R6D
SITE
2008
A–RB
A–R3D
A–Wck
A–R6D
A–R7
EXPLANATION
Unsuitable substrate
Microalgae
Other macroalgae
Cladophora (macroalgae)
Moss
Macrophytes

Figure 14. Average composition of aquatic plant communities by year, Fish Creek, Wyoming, 2007–08.

RPS bucket used to determine aquatic plant communities. Photograph by Cheryl A. Eddy-Miller.

of *Cladophora* between years are not known but could be related to the differences in timing and volume of streamflow between the years.

The relative abundance of macrophytes in the aquatic plant community generally increased from summer to fall at all of the sites with perennial flow during 2007 (fig. 15). For example, at sites A-R3D, A-Wck, and A-R6D, the proportion of macrophytes increased from July through October, after spring runoff occurred in June. High flows during spring runoff presumably were able to break and dislodge macrophytes, but after spring runoff, the macrophytes were able to grow and become more common in the aquatic plant community. In 2008, the proportion of macrophytes increased from summer to fall at site A-R6D but varied inconsistently at other sites (fig. 15).

The seasonal increase in the proportion of macrophytes in 2007 generally corresponded with decreases in the proportion of microalgae and unsuitable substrate (fig. 15). The proportion of macrophytes was negatively correlated with the proportions of microalgae ($r = -0.63$, $p = < 0.01$) and unsuitable habitat ($r = -0.40$, $p = 0.08$). The negative correlations likely indicate the seasonal growth of macrophytes covered areas that would otherwise have been classified as microalgae or unsuitable substrate.

True aquatic moss was relatively common at site A-R7, where moss composed as much as 36 percent of the aquatic plant community, and at site A-RB, where moss composed a smaller proportion of the community but was noted during nearly all of the sample visits. Mosses commonly are associated with small headwater streams and aerated waters with high concentrations of carbon dioxide (Hynes, 1970).

Aquatic Plant Community Production

Concentrations of dissolved oxygen in water were measured continuously on a diel basis for this study as presented in the "Water-Quality Properties" section and were used as an indicator of primary productivity of the aquatic plant community (Sorenson and others, 1999). Concentrations of dissolved oxygen and values of pH increased during the daylight hours (tables 11–18; example graph shown in fig. 16) as a result of photosynthesis by the algae, macrophytes, and moss present in the stream. The linear part of the dissolved-oxygen curve (fig. 16) was used to compute P_{max}, the maximum rate of productivity, by using the technique of Sorenson and others (1999). The difference between the maximum and minimum dissolved-oxygen concentrations over the linear part was divided by the number of hours in the linear part, to obtain an average value of P_{max} for each day, and the average P_{max} values for each day were averaged for each sampling period (table 6). The value of P_{max} is a relative measure of stream metabolism because the technique of Sorenson and others (1999) does not account for the effect of reaeration arising from differences in oxygen saturation between the stream and the atmosphere (Odum, 1956). The P_{max} is offset by respiration of the aquatic

community and decomposition of organic matter, which takes place 24 hours per day (Bott, 2006).

Respiration can be measured using various techniques such as calculating the rate of decrease in dissolved-oxygen concentrations during the predawn hours (Peterson and others, 2001). Respiration rates were not calculated for Fish Creek because the predawn concentrations of dissolved oxygen in Fish Creek generally increased instead of decreasing as expected, perhaps due to reaeration of the water across riffles.

Values of P_{max} in Fish Creek during 2007–08 ranged from 0.39 milligram per liter per hour (mg/L/hr) at site A-RB in May 2007, to 1.43 mg/L/hr at site A-R3D, also in May 2007 (table 6). The values of P_{max} listed by site and date in table 6 were calculated by averaging P_{max} from each of the two or three diel cycles available from each site in each sampling period. Considerable variability was noted among the sites and dates, although site A-R3D had the highest average of 0.82 mg/L/hr, compared to an average of about 0.70 mg/L/hr at the other sites on Fish Creek (table 6). For comparison, values of P_{max} in the Yellowstone River in Montana and Wyoming generally were less than 0.40 mg/L/hr, with the exception of one site associated with nuisance algal conditions where P_{max} reached 0.61 mg/L/hr (Peterson and others, 2001).

The rate of dissolved-oxygen production appeared to increase with progression of seasons in both 2007 and 2008. Average values of P_{max} for the surface-water sites by sampling date generally increased from March to October 2007 and from May to October 2008 (fig. 17). The increase in productivity from spring to summer can be at least partially attributed to increasing water temperatures that accelerate biological processes, but water temperatures declined between August and October (see figs. 6, 30–32), indicating the influence of other, unknown factors that caused P_{max} to reach a maximum in October of both years. Streamflow also declined between August and October in both years (fig. 4).

Algal Communities

Concentration data for chlorophyll-*a*, which is one of the primary photosynthetic pigments in algal cells (Graham and Wilcox, 2000), and ash-free dry mass (AFDM), which is a measure of organic matter including algae, bacteria, fungi, and other organisms, in algae samples collected during 2007–08 are available in table 7 and on the Web (U.S. Geological Survey, 2010a). The algal taxonomic identification data were used to characterize algal community traits and are available on the Web (U.S. Geological Survey, 2010b).

Algal Standing Crop

Concentrations of chlorophyll-*a* and AFDM, cell density, and cell biovoume are indicators of algal standing crop. Concentrations of chlorophyll-*a* tended to be higher at the sites with perennial flow than at sites with seasonal flow (table 7). Chlorophyll-*a* concentrations at the two sampling sites farthest upstream, sites A-R1U and A-R1D with seasonal

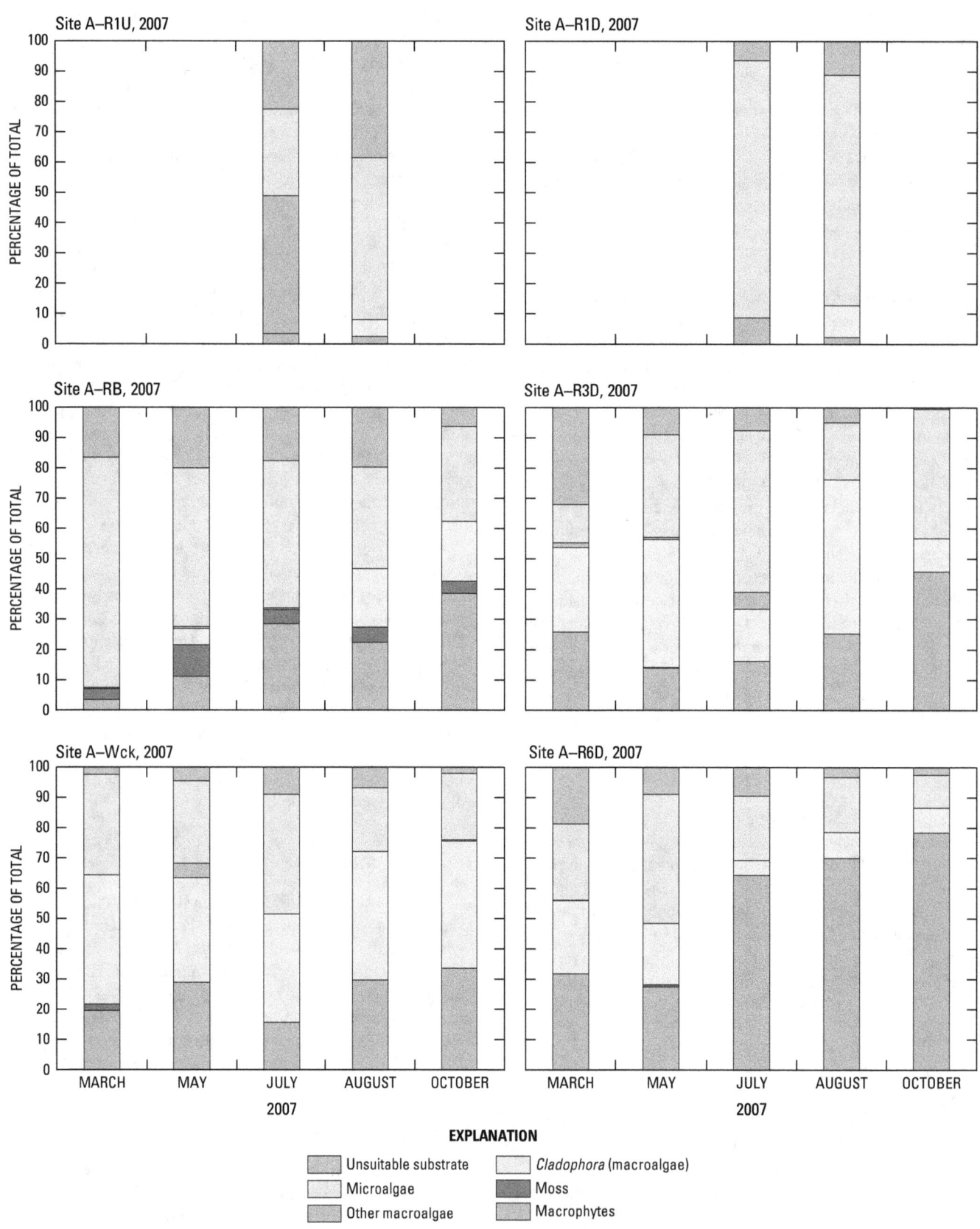

Figure 15.   Seasonal variation in aquatic plant community composition at sites on Fish Creek, Wyoming, 2007–08.

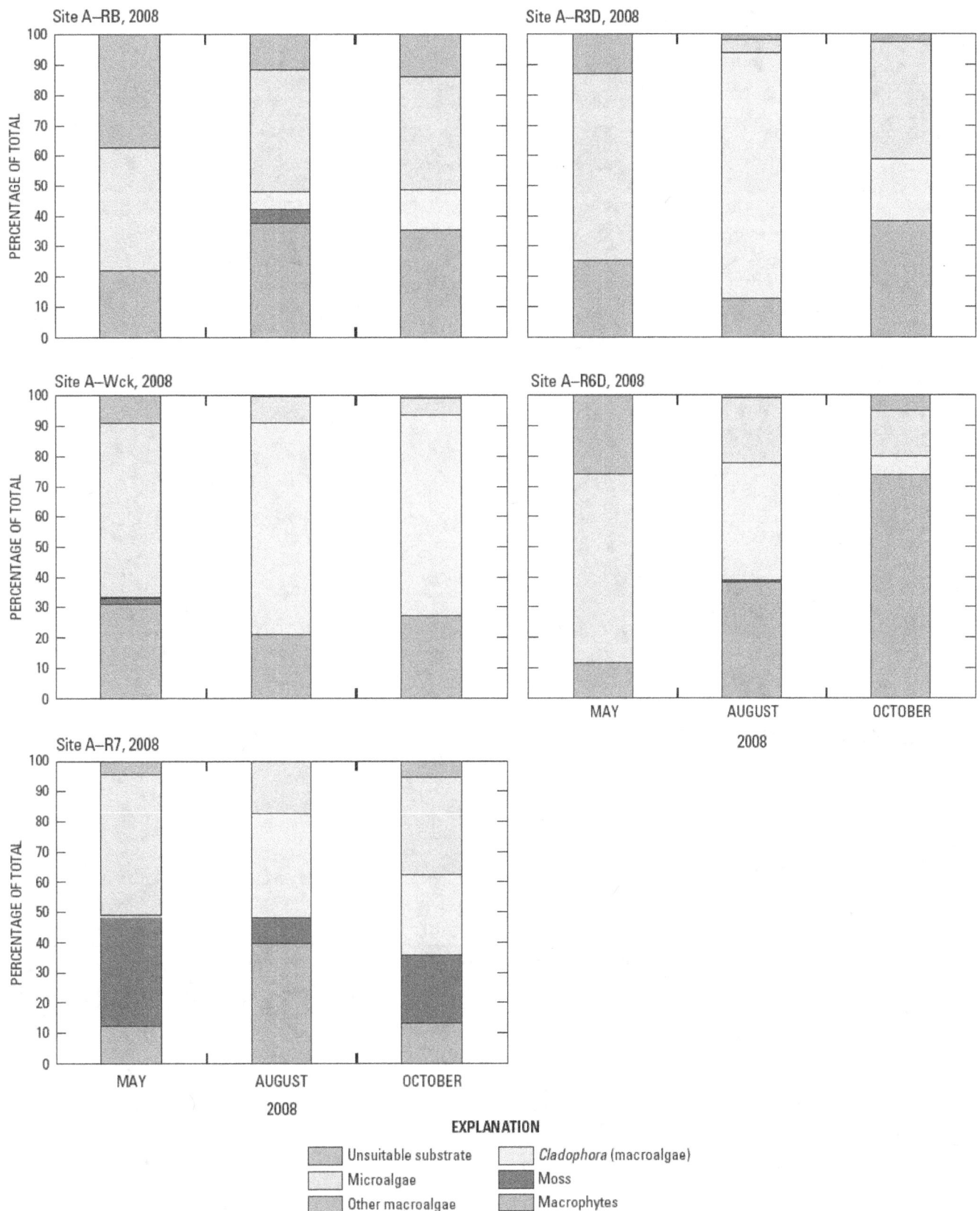

Figure 15.   Seasonal variation in aquatic plant community composition at sites on Fish Creek, Wyoming, 2007–08.—Continued

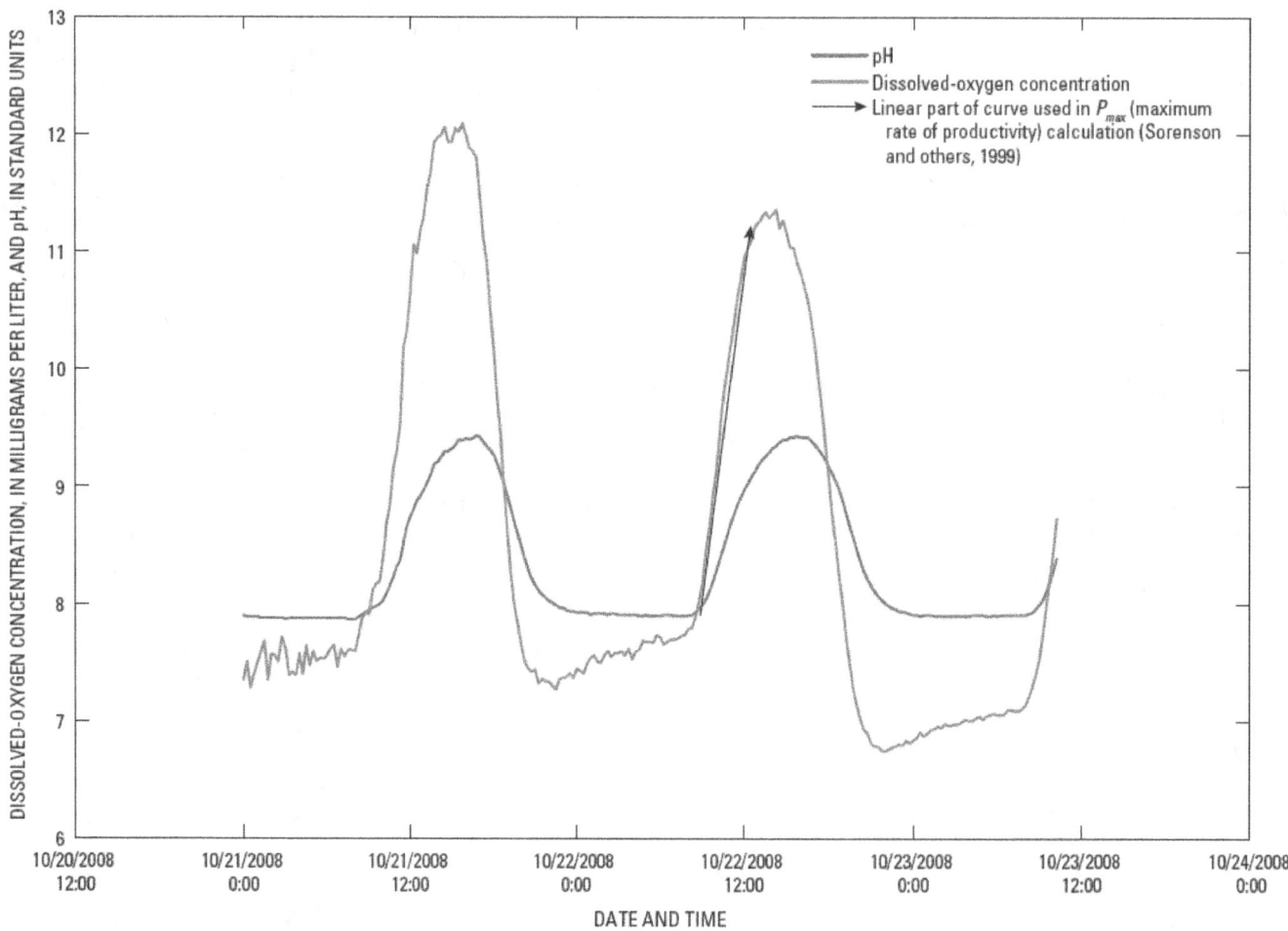

Figure 16. Diel fluctuations in dissolved-oxygen concentration and pH in Fish Creek at Wilson (Site A-Wck), Wyoming, October 21–23, 2008.

Table 6. Maximum rate of dissolved-oxygen production, P_{max}, in milligrams per liter per hour, Fish Creek, Wyoming, 2007–08.

[NA, not available or not applicable]

Site name	March 2007	May 2007	July 2007	August 2007	October 2007	May 2008	August 2008	October 2008	Average by site
A-RB	1.06	0 39	0.58	0.77	1.1	NA	0.42	0.60	0.70
A-R3D	.46	1.43	.78	.76	1 17	0.55	.69	.73	.82
A-WCK	.58	NA	.56	.94	.75	.76	.68	.76	.72
A-R6D	.47	53	NA	.80	.74	.63	.72	.99	.70
A-R7	NA	NA	NA	NA	NA	.50	.83	.66	.66
Average by date	.64	.78	.64	.82	94	.61	.67	.75	NA

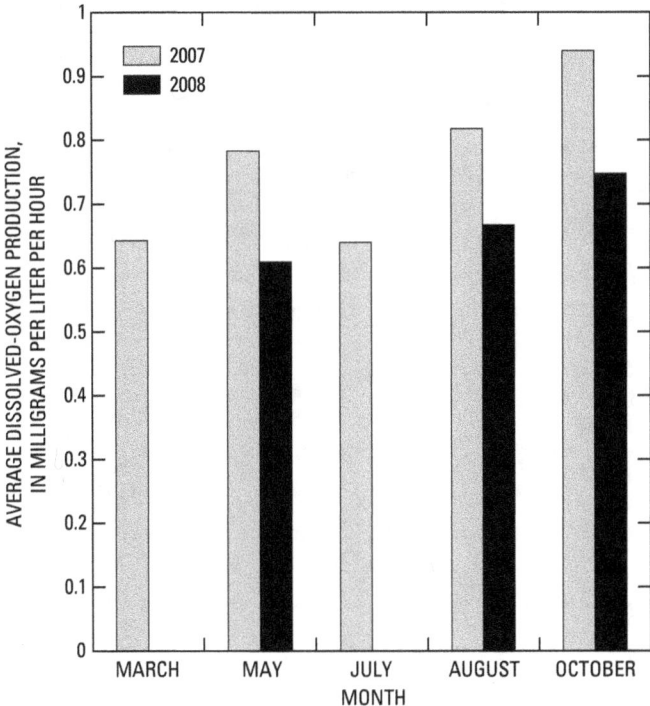

Figure 17. Seasonal change in average values of maximum rate of dissolved-oxygen production, P_{max}, at surface-water sites Fish Creek, Wyoming, 2007–08.

flow, were highly variable but averaged less than 200 milligrams per square meter (mg/m²) in 2007 (fig. 18). In contrast, chlorophyll-a concentrations at the sites with perennial flow, sites A-RB, A-R3D, A-Wck, and A-R6D, averaged greater than 200 mg/m². The highest average chlorophyll-a concentration in 2007 was at site A-R6D, which had an average of 341 mg/m². The average chlorophyll-a concentrations tended to be slightly higher in 2008 than in 2007 at all sites, with the exception of site A-Wck, which had notably higher chlorophyll-a concentrations in 2008 than in 2007. The average chlorophyll-a concentration of 1,480 mg/m² at site A-Wck in 2008 (fig. 18) was influenced by an extremely high concentration in October (table 7). Although the concentration for the October sample from site A-Wck was confirmed by re-analysis at the laboratory, the value probably should be considered as an outlier. Concentrations of chlorophyll-a at site A-R7, which was sampled only in 2008, were most similar to those in the upper part of Fish Creek at site A-RB.

Average concentrations of chlorophyll-a were smallest in the spring months of March and May, and largest in October 2007 (fig. 18). The chlorophyll-a concentrations during 2008 also indicated a seasonal peak in October. The seasonal peaks of chlorophyll-a concentrations are similar to the seasonal peak of P_{max} during October of 2007 and 2008 as described previously in the section "Aquatic Plant Community Production." Although the seasonal peaks of chlorophyll-a concentrations and P_{max} in Fish Creek during October seem late in the year, given that water temperatures were lower in October than

August, other work in the Rocky Mountain region (Lohman and Priscu, 1992) also has indicated substantial activity of algae well into October.

Concentrations of chlorophyll-a in Fish Creek consistently were high compared to values from other investigations. For example, in response to nuisance growths of *Cladophora* in the Clark Fork in Montana, local governments and industry agreed to voluntary upper limits of chlorophyll-a at 100 mg/m² averaged over the growing season and a peak concentration of 150 mg/m² (Watson and others, 2000). Ninety percent of the chlorophyll-a concentrations from Fish Creek exceeded 100 mg/m², and 75 percent exceeded 150 mg/m² (table 7). Almost all of the chlorophyll-a concentrations from Fish Creek were in the range of, or exceeded, the 100- to 200-mg/m² range suggested as an indicator of nuisance algal conditions by the U.S. Environmental Protection Agency (2000).

Concentrations of chlorophyll-a in Fish Creek also were considerably higher than historical data from other streams in the area (U.S. Geological Survey, 2010a). The average chlorophyll-a concentration of two samples from the Snake River near Flagg Ranch (station 13010065) in 2002–04 was 16 mg/m²; the average chlorophyll-a concentration of two samples collected from the Snake River at Moose, Wyo. (station 13013650) in 1996–97 was 1.7 mg/m². A sample collected from the Salt River near Etna (station 13027500) in 1993 had a chlorophyll-a concentration of 1.1 mg/m².

The AFDM concentrations in the algae samples were correlated with the chlorophyll-a concentrations ($r = 0.87$, $p = < 0.01$). The AFDM concentrations ranged from 9 grams per square meter (g/m²) at site A-R1U in May 2007 to 662 g/m² at site A-Wck in October 2008 (table 7). During 2007–08, AFDM concentrations generally were highest at site A-Wck, which had an average AFDM concentration of 209 g/m².

In 2007, algal density and biovolume generally peaked in July at all of the sites (table 7). Maximum densities exceeded 10 million cells per square centimeter (cells/cm²) at sites A-R3D and A-R6D in July 2007, and the densities were less than 2 million cells/cm² at those sites in March 2007 (table 7). Algal biovolume also peaked at sites A-R3D and A-R6D in July, at more than 6,000 cubic centimeters per square meter (cm³/m²). Although algal density and biovolume were moderately correlated with each other ($r = 0.70$, $p = < 0.01$), they were not correlated with either chlorophyll-a or AFDM. Algal samples were collected in 2008 for taxonomic identification and enumeration, but those samples had not been analyzed as of the date of this report (2010).

Algal Community Composition

Samples for identification of algal taxonomy were collected in March, May, July, August, and October 2007 from the surface-water sites unless the sites were dry (table 2). A majority of the 199 algal taxa identified in the 2007 samples were diatoms (Bacillariophyta), composing an average of

Table 7.   Concentrations of chlorophyll-a and ash free dry mass, algal cell density, and algal cell biovolume, Fish Creek, Wyoming, 2007–08.

[mg, milligrams; m^2, square meter; g, grams; cm^2, square centimeter; cm^3, cubic centimeter; NA, not available]

Site name	Sampling date (month/day/year)	Chlorophyll-a (mg/m^2)	Ash-free dry mass (g/m^2)	Cell density (cells/cm^2)	Cell biovolume (cm^3/m^2)
A-R1U	05/10/2007	12	9	157,890	3.9
A-R1U	07/10/2007	388	64	1,865,235	3.6
A-R1U	08/13/2007	79	26	432,186	2.9
A-R1D	07/10/2007	197	52	6,179,701	52.8
A-R1D	08/14/2007	12	21	624,115	1.6
A-RB	03/08/2007	126	70	535,432	2.4
A-RB	05/08/2007	47	39	1,159,700	2.9
A-RB	07/11/2007	220	103	3,106,384	8.5
A-RB	08/15/2007	247	99	1,608,764	180.9
A-RB	10/22/2007	432	168	1,550,684	55.7
A-RB	05/06/2008	206	63	NA	NA
A-RB	08/19/2008	167	91	NA	NA
A-RB	10/20/2008	284	57	NA	NA
A-R3D	03/07/2007	170	70	640,515	5.0
A-R3D	05/09/2007	158	51	2,354,769	887.6
A-R3D	07/11/2007	197	230	10,737,673	7,568.2
A-R3D	08/14/2007	194	112	1,969,896	571.9
A-R3D	10/25/2007	382	123	6,498,746	33.1
A-R3D	05/07/2008	241	103	NA	NA
A-R3D	08/19/2008	582	303	NA	NA
A-R3D	10/21/2008	319	82	NA	NA
A-Wck	03/06/2007	170	76	1,671,489	543.8
A-Wck	05/08/2007	178	65	8,836,243	198.6
A-Wck	07/12/2007	182	78	1,190,474	628.0
A-Wck	08/15/2007	109	46	2,768,297	307.2
A-Wck	10/24/2007	499	331	539,694	135.6
A-Wck	05/07/2008	242	94	NA	NA
A-Wck	08/20/2008	644	322	NA	NA
A-Wck	10/22/2008	3,540	662	NA	NA
A-R6D	03/07/2007	137	47	1,819,143	471.6
A-R6D	05/07/2007	79	41	6,547,301	126.7
A-R6D	07/12/2007	274	172	10,256,649	6,408.9
A-R6D	08/16/2007	352	161	3,862,382	404.9
A-R6D	10/25/2007	863	227	1,591,140	19.4
A-R6D	05/08/2008	141	66	NA	NA
A-R6D	08/20/2008	565	278	NA	NA
A-R6D	10/22/2008	548	135	NA	NA
A-R7	05/08/2008	375	146	NA	NA
A-R7	08/21/2008	112	92	NA	NA
A-R7	10/22/2008	365	131	NA	NA

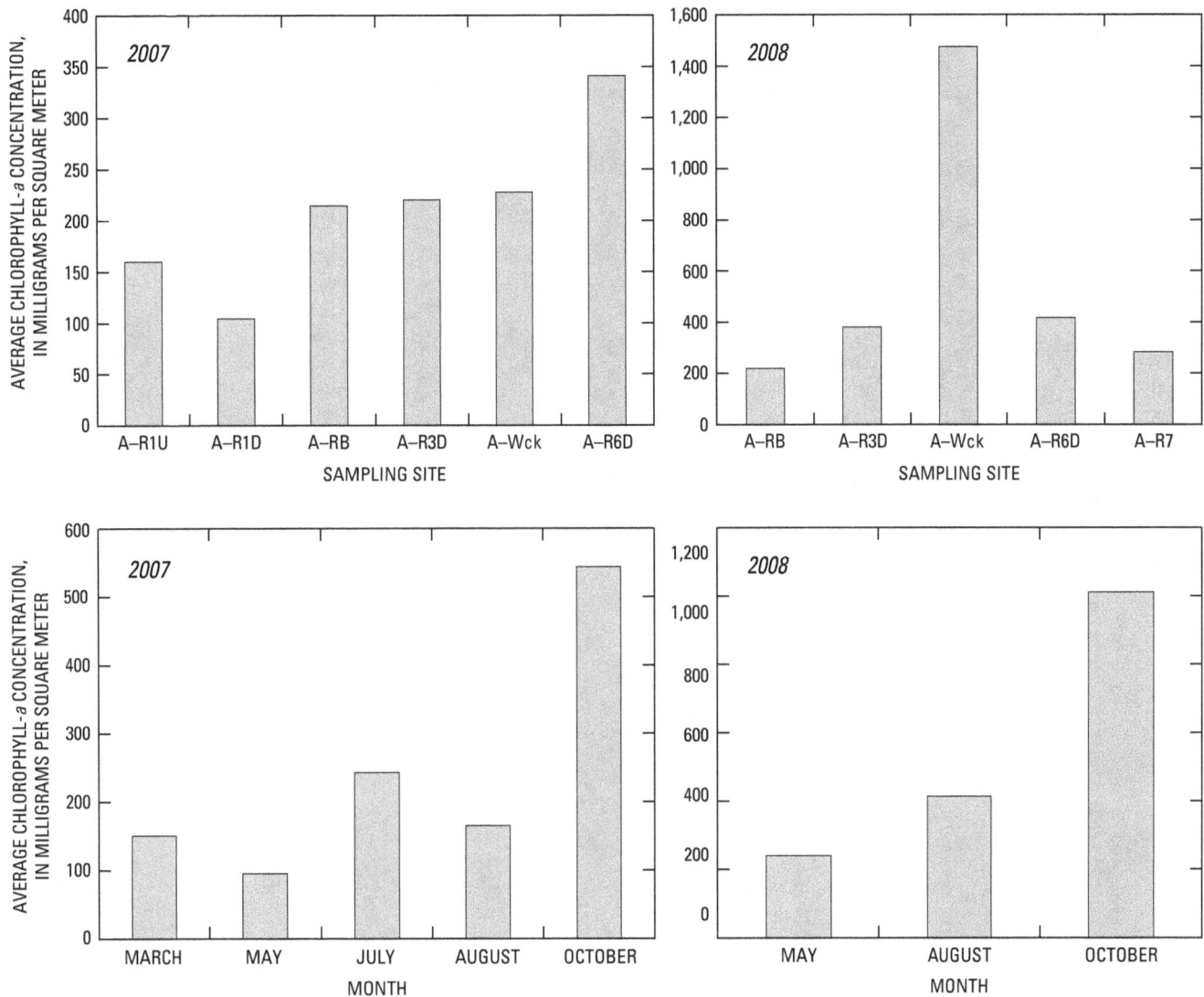

Figure 18. Average chlorophyll-*a* concentrations by season and by sampling site, Fish Creek, Wyoming, 2007–08.

87 percent of the total taxa richness by sample. Blue-green algae composed about 8 percent of the taxa richness, and green algae (Chlorophyta) composed about 4 percent of the taxa richness, on the average. In spite of having relatively few species, blue-green algae commonly were dominant in terms of density (average of 47 percent), and green algae commonly were dominant in terms of biovolume (average of 68 percent) at sites with perennial flow.

The taxonomic composition of the algal communities at the sites with seasonal flow (sites A-R1U and A-R1D) was notably different from the composition at sites with perennial flow (sites A-RB, A-R3D, A-Wck, and A-R6D). Nonmetric multidimensional scaling (NMDS) ordination showed two groups of sites with relatively similar taxonomic composition—one group composed of sites with seasonal flow and one group composed of sites with perennial flow (fig. 19*A*). Sites with seasonal flow contained an average of 31 algal

taxa per sample, whereas sites with perennial flow contained an average of 53 taxa per sample. Differences in community structure between sites with seasonal and perennial flow are likely due to streamflow conditions that allow overwintering of algal communities at the sites with perennial flow, whereas sites with seasonal flow are dry throughout the winter, meaning algal communities need to reestablish themselves when streamflow resumes in the spring or early summer. The quality-control samples (splits) collected from site A-R1U in July and from site A-R6D in October plotted relatively close to the corresponding environmental samples (fig. 19), indicating relatively high similarity of the quality-control samples to the environmental samples.

Predominant algal taxa, in terms of relative abundance, at site A-R1U were diatoms *Encyonema* subspecies (spp.) in May (35 percent of total density) and July (27 percent), green algae *Ulothrix* spp. in May (28 percent), blue-green algae

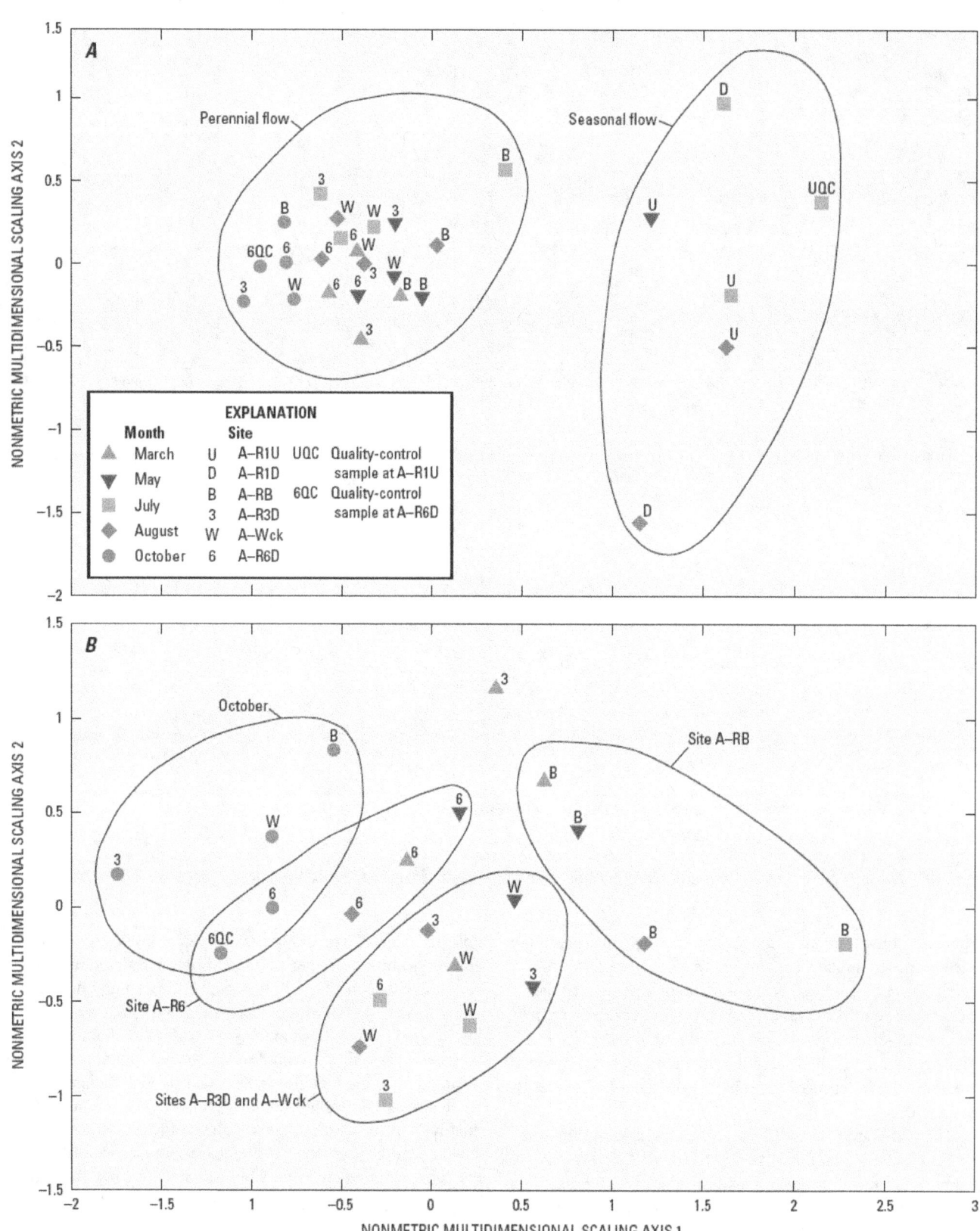

Figure 19.   Similarities of algal communities depicted by nonmetric multidimensional scaling ordination, Fish Creek, Wyoming, 2007. *A*, among all sites, and *B*, among sites with perennial flow.

Homoeothrix in July (24 percent) and August (15 percent), and blue-green algae *Phormidium* (26 percent) in August. Some of the same taxa also dominated in terms of biovolume in samples from site A-R1U, such as *Ulothrix* spp. in May (92 percent of total biovolume) and *Encyonema* spp. in July (36 percent). The July sample also contained the diatom *Synedra*, which constituted 23 percent of the biovolume. The green alga *Spirogyra* constituted 71 percent of the biovolume in the August sample from site A-R1U.

Predominant algal taxa at site A-R1D were the diatoms *Hydrurus foetidus* (relative abundance of 77 percent) in July and *Gomphonema* (19 percent) in August. The August sample also contained a number of blue-green algae taxa—*Homoeothrix*, *Phormidium* spp., and *Leptolyngbya*—that together made up 51 percent of the abundance. The biovolume of the July sample was dominated by *Ulothrix* spp. that constituted 80 percent of the total biovolume. The same three species of *Ulothrix* that dominated the biovolume of the July sample from site A-R1D also predominated in the May sample from site A-R1U. The biovolume of the August sample from site A-R1D was dominated by diatoms *Synedra* (27 percent) and *Gomphonema* (21 percent). Hynes (1970) noted that *Hydrurus*, *Ulothrix*, and *Phormidium* typically are cold-water species.

In order to better understand algal community composition, an NMDS ordination was performed using taxonomic data from only the sites with perennial flow (fig. 19B). That ordination indicated the algal communities had higher similarity by site than by date. For example, samples from site A-RB formed a group, indicating a stronger taxonomic similarity among samples collected in March through August at site A-RB than to samples from other sites. The samples from sites A-Wck and A-R3D formed a group, as did the samples from site A-R6D (fig. 19B). Samples from October tended to group together, an apparent exception to the pattern of higher similarity among samples from a given site. The similarity among algal communities in October might be a reflection of a shift in community composition in response to colder water and lower light intensity.

Blue-green algae were the most abundant algae on all five sample dates during March to October 2007 at site A-RB. One or more species of *Phormidium* predominated in all of the samples at as much as 50 percent of the relative abundance; *Leptolyngbya* was a subdominant species in the March sample, and *Homoeothrix* was a subdominant species in the July and August samples. The biovolume in samples from site A-RB was dominated by diatoms early in the year; *Gomphoneis* constituted 16 percent of the March sample and *Encyonema* constituted 27 percent of the May sample. Green algae constituted the bulk of the biovolume later in the year; *Ulothrix* dominated in July (69 percent), and *Cladophora* dominated in August and October (83 percent).

Blue-green algae predominated in terms of relative abundance at site A-R3D, similar to their dominance at sites A-RB, A-Wck, and A-R6D. The dominant algae at site A-R3D included *Phormidium tenue* in March (11 percent)

and May (24 percent), *Leibleinia* in July (19 percent) and August (16 percent), and *Homoethrix* and *Tolypothrix* in August (35 percent combined) and October (49 percent combined). The biovolume of the March sample from site A-R3D was dominated by the diatom *Didymosphenia geminata* (27 percent). This species is of particular interest because *Didymosphenia* is known for sometimes creating nuisance conditions in the United States and other areas of the world (*http://www.epa.gov/region8/water/didymosphenia/*). *Didymosphenia* also was identified in the samples from site A-RB in August and site A-R6D in March, at relatively low concentrations. The green algae *Cladophora* dominated the biovolume of the May, July, and August samples (98–99 percent) from site A-R3D; the diatoms *Cocconeis* and green algae *Ulothrix* dominated the biovolume in October. *Cladophora* was common in the aquatic plant community surveys described previously in this report and is well known for abundant growth and creating nuisance conditions in streams and lakes throughout the world (Whitton, 1970).

The predominant blue-green algae at site A-Wck included several taxa, such as *Heteroleibleinia*, *Leptolyngbya*, *Phormidium*, and *Tolypothrix,* that were common at other sites on Fish Creek. The blue-green algae *Nostoc* predominated in May (relative abundance 93 percent). *Nostoc* grows as cushion-like clumps and is known as a nitrogen fixer that is capable of fixing atmospheric nitrogen as a source of nutrients (Hynes, 1970). *Tolypothrix* and *Calothrix* (co-dominant at site A-R6D) also are known as nitrogen fixers, but the other species of blue-green algae common in Fish Creek are not known for nitrogen fixation (Porter, 2008). *Tolypothrix* was most abundant in August (75 percent) and October (20 percent). The biovolumes in all of the algal samples from site A-Wck were heavily dominated by *Cladophora* (96 to 99 percent).

At site A-R6D, blue-green algae such as *Heteroleibleinia*, *Chamaesiphon*, *Nostoc*, *Leptolyngbya*, *Leibleinia*, *Calothrix*, and *Phormidium* were the most abundant algae. Biovolume of the March, May, July, and August samples was dominated by *Cladophora* (93 to 99 percent). Biovolume of the October sample from A-R6D was dominated by the green algae *Mougeotia* (14 percent) and the diatom *Cymbella mexicana* (12 percent). *Cymbella* has a long, gelatinous stalk (Prescott, 1978) that can form mats superficially resembling the wooly brown-gray mats formed by *Didymosphenia* (M. Potapova, Academy of Natural Sciences Philadelphia, written commun., July 23, 2007).

Algal Community Traits

Algal community traits were calculated from genus or species-level autecological information (Porter, 2008) as potential indicators of nitrogen limitation, organic enrichment, sedimentation, and pH. Algal community traits for Fish Creek, based on relative abundance in 2007, are listed in table 8.

Nitrogen-fixing algae were present and sometimes dominant in the algal communities of Fish Creek. Nitrogen-fixing algae include diatoms in the family Rhopalodiaceae and blue-green algae that can fix atmospheric nitrogen as a nutrient

Table 8. Algal community traits, Fish Creek, Wyoming, 2007.

[Percentages may not sum to 100 percent due to rounding. >, greater than; <, less than]

Site name	Collection date	Nitrogen fixation (all algae)			Oxygen tolerance (diatoms)				Organic nitrogen (diatoms)		
		Nitrogen fixers (percent)	Not nitrogen fixers (percent)	Nitrogen fixation not classified (percent)	High (>75 percent saturation) (percent)	Moderately high (50–74 percent saturation) (percent)	Low (<50 percent saturation) (percent)	Unclassified (percent)	Nitrogen autotrophs (percent)	Nitrogen heterotrophs (percent)	Unclassified (percent)
A-R1U	05/10/2007	0	100	0	10	56	2	32	66	1	32
A-R1U	07/10/2007	0	100	0	12	28	3	57	35	5	59
A-R1U	08/13/2007	0	99	1	24	17	0	59	40	1	59
A-R1D	07/10/2007	0	100	0	36	18	1	45	52	3	46
A-R1D	08/14/2007	0	97	3	65	17	0	18	82	0	18
A-RB	03/08/2007	0	97	3	38	16	1	45	54	1	45
A-RB	05/08/2007	1	99	0	29	35	1	35	65	0	35
A-RB	07/11/2007	0	100	0	43	16	1	40	58	1	40
A-RB	08/15/2007	0	100	0	44	17	1	38	60	2	38
A-RB	10/22/2007	0	98	1	37	25	5	34	61	5	34
A-R3D	03/07/2007	0	93	7	44	15	3	38	58	4	38
A-R3D	05/09/2007	0	93	6	31	9	1	58	41	1	58
A-R3D	07/11/2007	3	69	29	38	9	0	52	47	0	52
A-R3D	08/14/2007	16	66	19	51	13	1	35	63	1	36
A-R3D	10/25/2007	24	74	2	43	20	2	35	62	3	35
A-Wck	03/06/2007	0	83	17	46	14	2	38	59	2	39
A-Wck	05/08/2007	93	7	0	39	9	1	50	49	1	50
A-Wck	07/12/2007	0	97	3	32	5	2	60	38	2	60
A-Wck	08/15/2007	78	20	2	47	17	1	35	64	1	35
A-Wck	10/24/2007	32	66	2	61	13	4	23	73	4	23
A-R6D	03/07/2007	0	86	14	47	16	2	35	63	2	35
A-R6D	05/07/2007	85	14	2	40	9	1	50	49	1	50
A-R6D	07/12/2007	0	82	17	39	12	3	46	51	3	46
A-R6D	08/16/2007	5	80	14	57	12	1	30	69	1	30
A-R6D	10/25/2007	8	78	14	50	14	0	36	63	1	36

Table 8. Algal community traits, Fish Creek, Wyoming, 2007.—Continued

[Percentages may not sum to 100 percent due to rounding. >, greater than; <, less than]

Site name	Collection date	Pollution class[1] (diatoms)			Motility (all algae)		Sediment (diatoms)	pH (diatoms)		
		Sensitive (percent)	Tolerant (percent)	Unclassified (percent)	Motile (percent)	Not motile (percent)	Increasers (percent)	Circumneutral (percent)	Alkaliphilic (percent)	Alkalibiontic (percent)
A-R1U	05/10/2007	68	17	15	11	89	6	75	12	0
A-R1U	07/10/2007	29	38	32	14	85	3	80	15	0
A-R1U	08/13/2007	41	16	43	35	65	4	77	15	0
A-R1D	07/10/2007	53	18	29	7	93	16	19	45	0
A-R1D	08/14/2007	34	3	63	31	67	7	22	71	0
A-RB	03/08/2007	46	23	31	14	83	42	25	45	5
A-RB	05/08/2007	61	7	32	28	72	29	51	35	0
A-RB	07/11/2007	52	16	33	50	50	36	24	57	0
A-RB	08/15/2007	56	17	26	54	46	36	24	65	0
A-RB	10/22/2007	56	27	17	24	75	40	16	62	1
A-R3D	03/07/2007	57	18	25	22	72	39	21	55	0
A-R3D	05/09/2007	39	16	45	30	63	27	19	37	1
A-R3D	07/11/2007	46	10	44	3	69	22	12	36	12
A-R3D	08/14/2007	62	18	20	8	73	26	16	49	8
A-R3D	10/25/2007	66	19	16	14	85	17	16	52	9
A-Wck	03/06/2007	58	18	24	7	76	38	25	58	1
A-Wck	05/08/2007	48	12	40	1	99	37	22	44	6
A-Wck	07/12/2007	37	11	52	24	73	26	15	41	2
A-Wck	08/15/2007	59	26	15	3	95	22	21	44	17
A-Wck	10/24/2007	66	23	11	10	88	14	11	52	21
A-R6D	03/07/2007	68	16	16	11	75	45	14	74	1
A-R6D	05/07/2007	48	10	42	4	95	34	32	46	5
A-R6D	07/12/2007	50	17	33	5	78	25	20	52	4
A-R6D	08/16/2007	65	23	11	19	67	39	10	62	10
A-R6D	10/25/2007	59	18	23	26	59	27	11	49	16

[1]Based on classification by Bahls (1993).

source and therefore have a competitive advantage when concentrations of nitrogen, a key nutrient for algae, in the water are low (Stevenson and others, 1996; Peterson and Grimm, 1992), or when ratios of nitrogen to phosphorus in water are low (Fairchild and others, 1985). The relative abundance of Rhopalodiaceae in Fish Creek generally increased seasonally and in the downstream direction (fig. 20). The maximum abundance of the Rhopalodiaceae occurred at sites A-R3D, A-Wck, and A-R6D in August and October 2007. The relative abundance of nitrogen fixers among all algae, including blue-green algae such as *Nostoc*, *Calothrix*, and *Tolypothrix*, was variable but tended to be highest at the same sites and dates as the Rhopalodiaceae (table 8). The variability in nitrogen fixers among all algae might be related to the colonial nature of the blue-green algae such as the cushion-shaped colonies of *Nostoc*.

Metrics for oxygen tolerance, organic nitrogen, and pollution class indicated relatively low organic enrichment in Fish Creek. Oxygen tolerance refers to the relative oxygenation of a stream such as one with relatively high amounts of organic enrichment (for example, sewage) and high biochemical oxygen demand, compared to a well-oxygenated stream with little organic enrichment (Porter, 2008; Van Dam and others, 1994). Diatoms associated with high dissolved-oxygen concentrations (greater than 75 percent saturation, table 8) and low organic enrichment generally predominated in Fish Creek, with smaller proportions of diatoms associated with moderate or low dissolved-oxygen concentrations. Metrics for organic nitrogen indicated the diatom communities were primarily nitrogen autotrophs that do not require high concentrations of organic nitrogen (Porter, 2008; Van Dam and others, 1994) (table 8). Nitrogen heterotrophs that are adapted to high concentrations of organic nitrogen, such as from sewage effluent, generally were uncommon in the diatom communities. Using pollution classes defined by Bahls (1993) for streams in Montana, the

diatom communities in Fish Creek were predominantly sensitive species (average relative abundance of 53 percent), with smaller percentages of tolerant species (average of 17 percent). The remainder of the species was unclassified with regard to pollution class (table 8).

Algal metrics for motility and sediment increasers indicated species capable of responding to sedimentation were most abundant at site A-RB. Algal motility generally was highest at site A-RB and lowest at site A-Wck (table 8). The motility metric is the relative abundance of all algae, such as those in the genera *Nitzchia* and *Navicula*, that have the ability to move in water or on submerged surfaces and thereby avoid sedimentation (Porter, 2008). Greater proportions of motile species generally indicate that the site is subject to greater sedimentation than sites with smaller proportions. Sites A-R1U and A-R1D, which had manmade stream channels, had average motility values of 20 and 19 percent, respectively. Site A-RB represents the most upstream site with a natural channel but had the highest proportion of motile species (average of 34 percent motility) of any of the sites on Fish Creek. The average motility metric values from the other sites were 15 percent for site A-R3D; 9 percent for site A-Wck; and 13 percent for site A-R6D. The proportion of sediment increasers, or those diatom species that increase in relative abundance in response to increases in sedimentation (Teply and Bahls, 2007), was highest at site A-RB (table 8). The relative abundance of sediment increasers averaged 37 percent at site A-RB, compared to 26 percent at site A-R3D, 28 percent at site A-Wck, and 34 percent at site A-R6D. The relative abundance of sediment increasers in the diatom community generally decreased with season, from March to October, at sites A-R3D, A-Wck, and A-R6D. In contrast, values of the motility metric did not seem to have a seasonal pattern. The sediment increaser species from Teply and Bahls (2007) that occurred in highest proportions at site

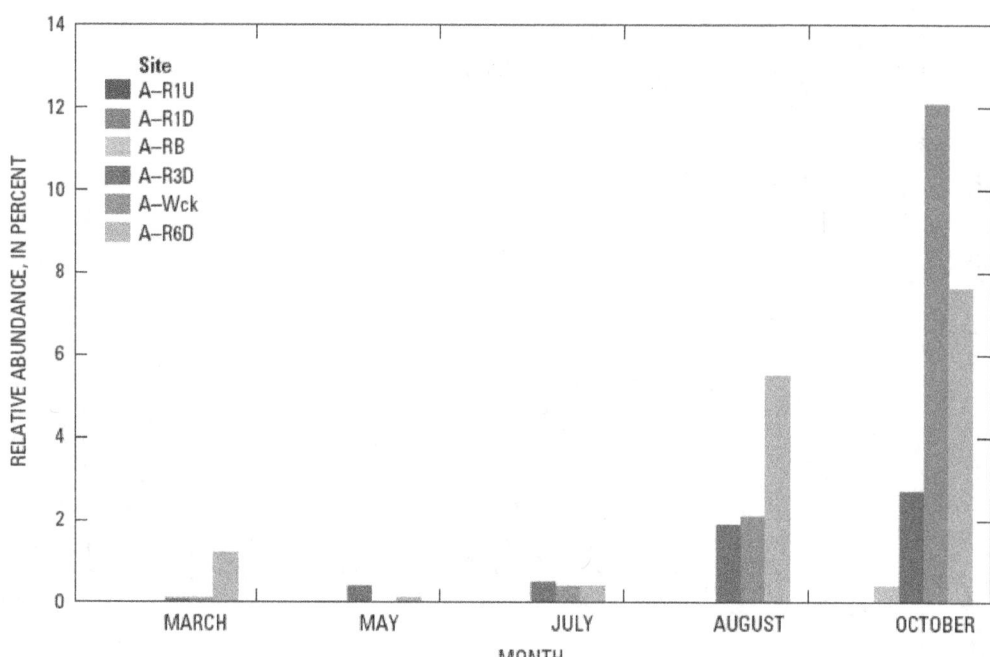

Figure 20. Relative abundance of nitrogen-fixing diatoms (Rhopalodiaceae) in algal communities of Fish Creek, Wyoming, 2007.

A-RB and other sites in Fish Creek were *Navicula tripunctata*, *Nitzchia fonticola*, and *Staurosirella leptostauron*. The source for the sedimentation at site A-RB indicated by the metrics is not known but might be related to the lower streamflow and smaller particle size in the pebble counts described in the "Streambed Substrate" section.

Algal communities in Fish Creek indicated increasing pH optima in the downstream direction. At site A-R1U, 75 to 80 percent of the diatom abundance was associated with circumneutral pH values near 7 (table 8). Sites farther downstream contained communities with higher percentages of alkaliphilic diatoms (pH generally greater than 7) and alkalibiontic diatoms (pH always greater than 7). A seasonal trend also was apparent; the alkalibiontic diatoms made up greater proportions of the community later in the season. For example the maximum proportions of alkalibiontic diatoms by site occurred in October at site A-Wck (21 percent) and site A-R6D (16 percent).

Macroinvertebrate Communities

Samples for identification of macroinvertebrate taxonomy were collected in May and August of 2007 and 2008 from the surface-water sites unless the sites were dry (table 2). Macroinvertebrate taxonomy data are available on the Web (U.S. Geological Survey, 2010b).

Macroinvertebrate Community Composition

Similar to the algal communities, the macroinvertebrate taxa richness was lower at the sites with seasonal streamflow, sites A-R1U and A-R1D, near Teton Village, than at the sites farther downstream with perennial flow. Taxa richness (table 9) averaged 22 taxa per sample at site A-R1U (May and August 2007) and was 28 taxa at site A-R1D (August 2007), compared to average taxa richness of 38 to 50 taxa per sample at sites A-RB, A-R3D, A-Wck, A-R6D, and A-R7 in 2007–08. Macroinvertebrate taxa richness was lower at the sites with seasonal flow than at the sites with perennial flow, likely due to a loss of habitat from winter drying and reduction of food sources such as algae, other aquatic plants, and organic matter. Macroinvertebrate samples were not collected from the sites with seasonal flow in 2008; therefore, the following characterization includes macroinvertebrate data from only the sites with perennial flow for the sake of comparability.

The Diptera (true flies) composed about one-half of the macroinvertebrate taxa identified in Fish Creek (fig. 21). Within the Diptera order, the family Chironomidae (midges) predominated and averaged about 18 taxa per sample. The Ephemeroptera (mayflies), Trichoptera (caddisflies), and Plecoptera (stoneflies), which are collectively known as the EPT, had smaller proportions of the overall community taxa richness than Diptera. The EPT were more common in May than August of both 2007 and 2008 (fig. 21 and table 9), indicating seasonal variation in community composition. Conversely, Diptera and noninsects had higher proportions of the

community taxa richness in August than May of both years. Noninsects were composed mostly of various taxa of Oligochaeta (worms) but also included Arachnida (mites), Crustacea (such as scuds), Mollusca (snails and fingernail clams), Nematoda (nematodes), and Turbellaria (flatworms) (U.S. Geological Survey, 2010b). A few taxa of Coleoptera (beetles) and Hemiptera (true bugs) were identified in the samples and are shown as other insects in figure 21. Odonata (dragonflies and damselflies) were not identified in any of the samples.

Seasonal variation in macroinvertebrate community composition in terms of density of the various taxa also occurred in conjunction with the seasonal variation in taxa richness. An NMDS ordination of the taxonomic data showed two groups of samples, the May samples and the August samples (fig. 22). The grouping by sample period indicated relatively high similarity among samples collected during May 2007 to those collected during May 2008, and high similarity among samples collected during August 2007 to those from August 2008. The differences in the macroinvertebrate communities between May and August were due largely to differences in taxa richness and abundance of Ephemeroptera and Trichoptera compared to Diptera and noninsects. Macroinvertebrate communities of Fish Creek contained more Ephemeroptera and Trichoptera in May than in August during both 2007 and 2008. Interannual variation was a smaller contributing factor as indicated by the general position of the 2007 samples near the top of the May and August groups and the position of the 2008 samples near the bottom of the groups in figure 22. Downstream changes in community composition also can be inferred from the position of samples from site A-RB (site farthest upstream) near the top of the May and August groups, and the position of site A-R7 (site farthest downstream) near the bottom of each group in figure 22. Communities at the intermediate sites A-R3D, A-Wck, and A-R6D tended to be similar to each other within the May and August groups.

Ephemeroptera (mayflies) accounted for about 20–50 percent of the relative abundance of macroinvertebrates in the May 2007 and 2008 samples (fig. 23). The dominant taxa of Ephemeroptera in May were *Baetis tricaudatus* and *Ephemerella* (U.S. Geological Survey, 2010b). Several taxa of Ephemeroptera were identified in the May samples but not in August samples, including *Ephemerella*, *Epeorus*, and *Cinygmula* (U.S Geological Survey, 2010b). Some of the Ephemeroptera taxa present in May persisted into August, including *Baetis tricaudatus*, which composed 26 percent of the relative abundance at site A-R7 and 17 percent at site A-R6D in August.

Plecoptera were uncommon in Fish Creek and generally were present in May but not August. The maximum abundance of Plecoptera occurred in May 2007, when *Isoperla* composed 8 percent of the community at site A-RB. Trichoptera composed 11–22 percent of the macroinvertebrates in May and 3–17 percent in August of 2007–08. The most common taxa of Trichoptera were *Amiocentrus aspilus*, particularly in May, *Brachycentrus spp.*, and various genera of Hydropsychidae.

Table 9. Macroinvertebrate community metrics, Fish Creek, Wyoming, 2007–08.

[m², meters squared]

Station number	Station name	Sample collection date (month/day/year)	Taxa richness							Density (numbers/m²)	Taxa relative abundance (in percent)							Functional group richness					
			Total	Ephemeroptera (mayflies)	Plecoptera (stoneflies)	Trichoptera (caddisflies)	Diptera (true flies)	Chironomidae (midges)	Non-insects		Ephemeroptera (mayflies)	Plecoptera (stoneflies)	Trichoptera (caddisflies)	Diptera (true flies)	Chironomidae (midges)	Non-insects	Predator taxa	Omnivore scraper taxa	Collector-gatherer taxa	Filterer-collector taxa	Scraper taxa	Shredder taxa
433505110494001	A-R1U	05/10/2007	15	1	0	1	9	8	3	859	49	0	0	46	46	4	1	0	11	2	1	0
433505110494001	A-R1U	08/13/2007	30	2	1	1	20	16	5	476	1	0	0	93	91	6	4	0	21	1	2	2
433438110495901	A-R1D	08/14/2007	28	2	0	0	18	16	6	390	1	0	0	81	74	17	2	1	21	1	2	0
433302110504701	A-RB	05/08/2007	35	6	2	11	11	9	3	448	23	8	21	46	46	1	4	0	17	4	6	3
433302110504701	A-RB	08/15/2007	37	3	0	5	23	19	5	1363	1	0	3	81	78	16	3	2	22	4	3	2
433302110504701	A-RB	05/06/2008	45	6	1	8	19	17	9	2040	23	1	22	48	47	4	5	1	22	7	6	3
433302110504701	A-RB	08/19/2008	37	4	0	5	17	15	8	2306	3	0	3	89	88	3	4	1	22	4	3	1
433117110515101	A-R3D	05/09/2007	48	7	3	13	19	15	5	252	51	1	14	33	31	1	9	1	18	9	5	4
433117110515101	A-R3D	08/14/2007	35	1	1	5	21	18	5	538	2	0	10	79	74	8	6	2	14	8	1	3
433117110515101	A-R3D	05/07/2008	50	6	2	11	23	19	6	3120	32	0	13	37	34	16	7	1	19	10	6	4
433117110515101	A-R3D	08/19/2008	48	2	0	6	24	21	14	557	2	0	7	72	66	17	5	0	24	8	5	4
13016450	A-Wck	05/08/2007	43	6	2	10	19	17	4	129	47	0	18	32	32	2	4	1	17	7	8	6
13016450	A-Wck	08/15/2007	46	1	0	8	26	21	10	507	7	0	13	53	49	27	9	2	16	8	3	6
13016450	A-Wck	05/07/2008	50	7	4	8	18	14	10	1123	41	1	13	32	29	11	9	0	16	9	6	6
13016450	A-Wck	08/20/2008	54	3	0	6	27	24	14	302	8	0	3	57	55	29	5	2	28	8	3	5
432906110522601	A-R6D	05/07/2007	50	7	3	11	19	16	6	300	40	4	13	37	36	2	9	3	19	8	5	6
432906110522601	A-R6D	08/16/2007	46	2	0	6	26	23	8	845	7	0	6	74	66	11	5	3	20	8	4	4
432906110522601	A-R6D	05/08/2008	46	6	2	7	20	17	9	945	41	0	18	29	26	8	5	0	18	9	5	6
432906110522601	A-R6D	08/20/2008	48	3	0	7	21	19	13	750	18	0	5	63	61	12	5	0	26	8	4	3
432748110515301	A-R7	05/08/2008	52	6	1	9	20	17	14	2560	19	0	11	41	38	21	8	0	21	9	7	4
432748110515301	A-R7	08/21/2008	49	3	1	7	19	16	15	566	28	0	17	33	28	11	7	2	20	7	6	5

Table 9. Macroinvertebrate community metrics, Fish Creek, Wyoming, 2007-08.—Continued

[m², meters squared]

Station number	Station name	Sample collection date (month/day/year)	Functional group relative abundance (in percent)						Tolerance score	Tolerance group relative abundance (in percent)		
			Predator taxa	Omnivore scraper taxa	Collector-gatherer taxa	Filterer-collector taxa	Scraper	Shredder		Intolerant macroinvertebrates	Moderately tolerant macroinvertebrates	Tolerant macroinvertebrates
433505110494001	A-R1U	05/10/2007	0	0	97	0	2	0	5.7	53	19	28
433505110494001	A-R1U	08/13/2007	1	0	87	2	10	0	5.5	35	49	16
433438110495901	A-R1D	08/14/2007	1	0	85	6	7	0	6.0	3	82	15
433302110504701	A-RB	05/08/2007	8	0	75	7	9	0	3.9	65	30	5
433302110504701	A-RB	08/15/2007	1	1	83	3	2	8	4.8	23	39	38
433302110504701	A-RB	05/06/2008	5	1	80	7	6	1	4.6	50	28	22
433302110504701	A-RB	08/19/2008	1	0	92	1	2	3	5.0	32	44	24
433117110515101	A-R3D	05/09/2007	2	0	81	11	3	1	3.8	77	19	4
433117110515101	A-R3D	08/14/2007	3	1	56	25	0	9	4.8	26	50	23
433117110515101	A-R3D	05/07/2008	4	0	60	16	3	3	4.1	50	26	24
433117110515101	A-R3D	08/19/2008	6	0	68	17	1	4	5.5	23	52	25
13016450	A-Wck	05/08/2007	2	0	76	11	5	6	4.1	72	25	3
13016450	A-Wck	08/15/2007	4	1	41	26	1	12	5.3	26	35	39
13016450	A-Wck	05/07/2008	10	0	68	13	5	3	4.2	64	19	17
13016450	A-Wck	08/20/2008	4	0	70	8	3	12	5.4	16	51	32
432906110522601	A-R6D	05/07/2007	7	0	75	8	5	5	4.0	68	22	10
432906110522601	A-R6D	08/16/2007	3	2	53	25	1	9	5.3	25	41	35
432906110522601	A-R6D	05/08/2008	5	0	76	10	4	3	4.5	67	19	14
432906110522601	A-R6D	08/20/2008	2	0	76	9	2	8	5.4	29	46	25
432748110515301	A-R7	05/08/2008	4	0	59	11	9	6	4.8	40	29	31
432748110515301	A-R7	08/21/2008	6	1	54	20	11	5	5.3	66	22	12

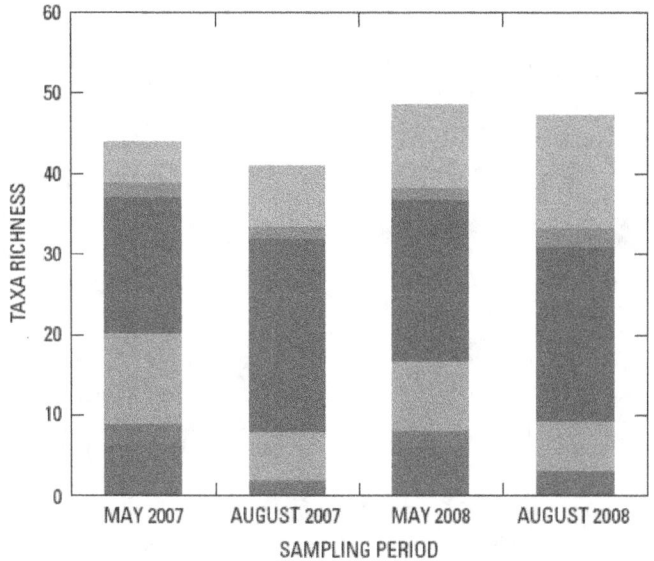

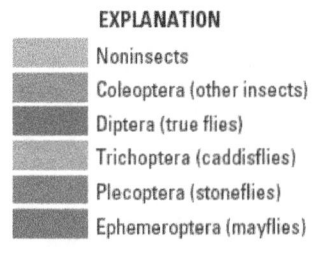

Figure 21. Average taxa richness of macroinvertebrate communities by sampling period for sites with perennial flow, Fish Creek, Wyoming, 2007–08.

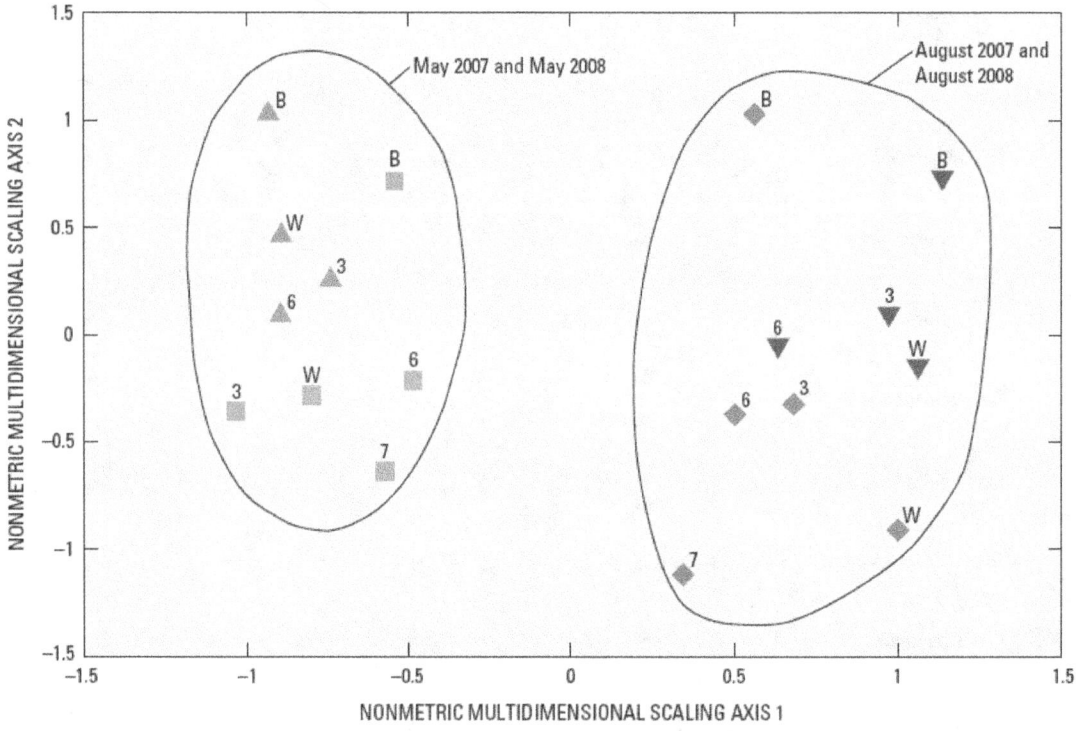

Figure 22. Similarities of macroinvertebrate communities depicted by nonmetric multidimensional scaling ordination for sites with perennial flow, Fish Creek, Wyoming, 2007–08.

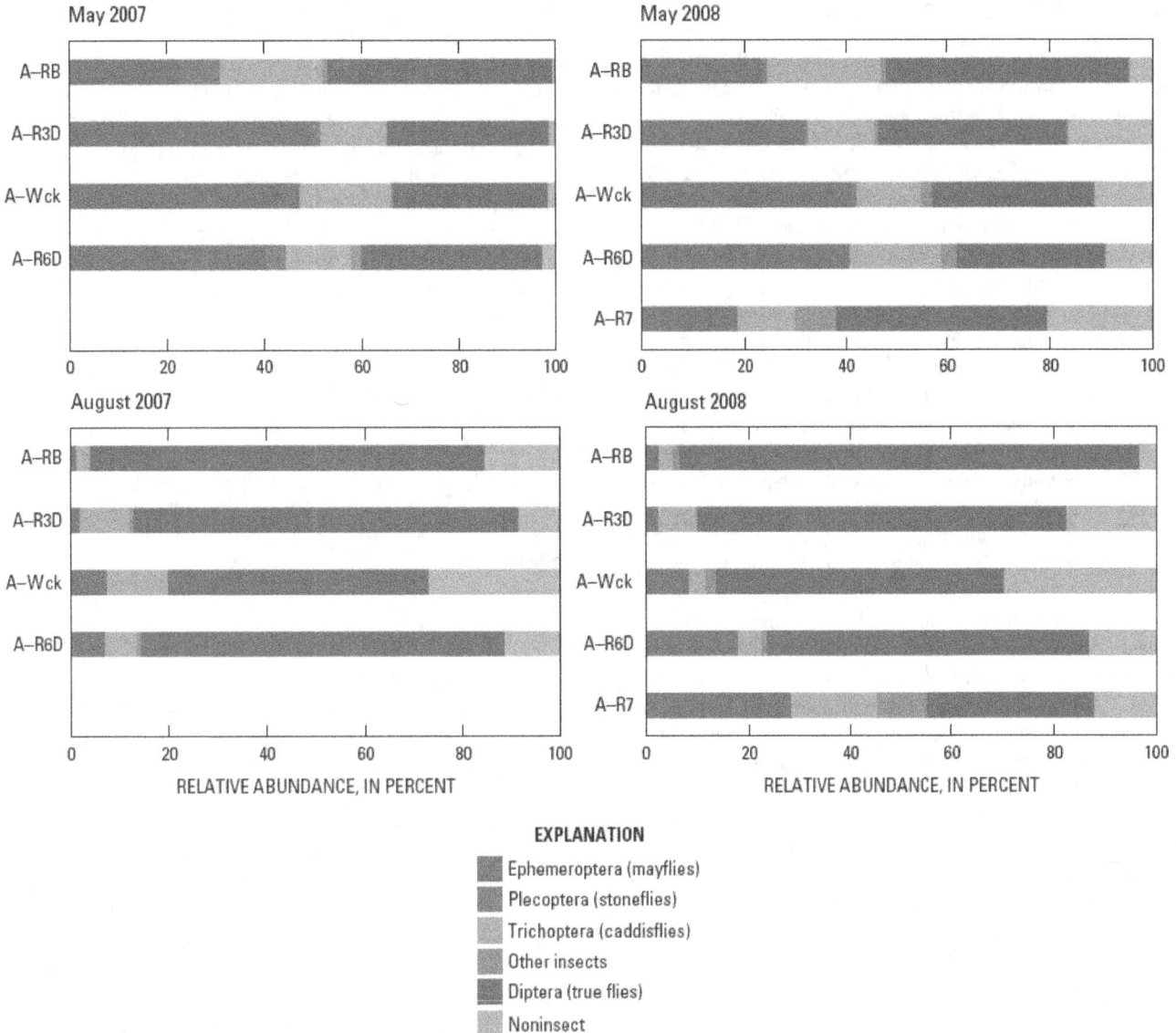

Figure 23.   Relative abundance of macroinvertebrate taxonomic groups at sites with perennial flow, Fish Creek, Wyoming, 2007–08.

Diptera were common in both May and August 2007–08 but were more common in the August samples (fig. 23). Chironomidae composed 26–47 percent of the total macroinvertebrate abundance (average of 36 percent) in May, and 28–88 percent (average of 63 percent) in August. The most common taxa of Chironomids were *Cricotopus/Orthocladius*, *Pagastia*, and *Eukiefferiella* in both May and August of 2007–08.

Noninsects identified from Fish Creek included several species of *Nais* (Oligochaeta), which are aquatic counterparts to the terrestrial earthworm (Pennak, 1978). The *Nais* spp. and other noninsects reached maximum relative abundance at site A-Wck, where noninsects composed 27 percent in August 2007 and 29 percent in August 2008 (table 9; fig. 23).

Generally, the EPT are considered indicators of favorable water quality, and their proportions decrease in response to increasing perturbation (Barbour and others, 1999). The proportion of organisms tolerant of degraded water quality, such as many of the Diptera and noninsects, is expected to increase with increasing perturbation (Barbour and others, 1999). Although the seasonal change in macroinvertebrate community composition in Fish Creek indicates a shift toward more tolerant taxa later in the year, this change might be due to factors other than water quality, such as the change in algal communities.

Macroinvertebrate Community Traits

Functional feeding group and tolerance of the macroinvertebrate communities were examined as traits or indicators of community dynamics. Functional feeding groups indicate feeding preferences on the basis of classifying macroinvertebrates into various groups such as collector-gatherers, scrapers, shredders, filterer-collectors, and predators (Barbour and others, 1999). Tolerance represents relative sensitivity to perturbation from various stressors such as organic pollution and sedimentation (Barbour and others, 1999).

Functional feeding groups of macroinvertebrate communities in Fish Creek shifted substantially with season in 2007–08. Although most of the macroinvertebrates in Fish Creek were classified as collector-gatherers, the relative abundance of collector-gatherers, scrapers, and predators was notably higher in the May samples than the August samples (fig. 24). Macroinvertebrates in the collector-gatherer feeding group include the mayfly *Baetis tricaudatus*, for example, that was common in both May and August. The difference in relative abundance of scrapers between May and August was significant (Wilcoxon rank-sum test, p<0.05). Scraper taxa that were common in the May samples but not August include the Ephemeroptera *Epeorus* and *Cinygmula*. The seasonal decrease in relative abundance of the macroinvertebrate scraper feeding group might be related to the seasonal change in aquatic plant communities. Merritt and Cummins (1996) describe scrapers as grazing scrapers on mineral and organic surfaces. The mineral surfaces in Fish Creek are the rock surfaces that were characterized as containing microalgae during the aquatic plant community surveys. The decrease in microalgae surfaces from May to August, as described previously in the "Aquatic Plant Community Composition" section of this report, might be a factor in the decrease of macroinvertebrate scrapers. The Plecoptera, such as *Isoperla,* which are predators, were most common in May and virtually absent during August, which helps explain the seasonal decrease in the predator feeding group in Fish Creek (fig. 24).

Conversely, the relative abundance of the shredder and filterer-collector feeding groups was higher in August than in May (fig. 24). The difference in relative abundance of shredders between May and August was significant (Wilcoxon rank sum test [Helsel and Hirsch, 1992], p<0.05). An example of a macroinvertebrate taxon in the shredder feeding group is the Chironomid *Cricotopus* that was more common in August than in May. Merritt and Cummins (1996) describe *Cricotopus* as an inhabitant of vascular hydrophytes and algal mats. The seasonal increase in relative abundance of *Cricotopus* is consistent with the seasonal increase in macrophytes and *Cladophora* in Fish Creek that was described previously in the "Aquatic Plant Community Composition" section of this report. Examples of filterer-collector taxa that were more common in August than May include the Trichoptera *Brachycentrus occidentalis* and the blackfly larvae *Simulium*.

Macroinvertebrate communities in Fish Creek had substantially higher tolerance scores in August than in May. The median tolerance score based on taxa richness in the samples was 4.1 in May and 5.3 in August (fig. 25). The tolerance scores were based on a range of 0–10, from least to most perturbation or organic enrichment (Hilsenhoff, 1987; Cuffney, 2003). Tolerance scores also indicated a decrease in relative abundance of intolerant (score range of 0 to less than 4) macroinvertebrates from May to August (fig. 25). Concurrently, the relative abundance of moderately tolerant (range of 4 to less than 7), and tolerant (range of 7 to 10) macroinvertebrates increased from May to August. The differences in tolerance scores between May and August were significant at p<0.05 in a Wilcoxon rank-sum test for taxa richness and all three ranges of tolerance score.

Habitat Characteristics

Habitat characteristics of streambed substrate (pebble count) and riparian canopy were measured at the surface-water sites with perennial flow in 2008. Streambed substrate data were collected twice, and riparian canopy data were collected once.

Streambed Substrate

The streambed substrate was measured in May 2008, prior to the 2008 high flows, and in October 2008 (table 2). With the exception of the most upstream site on Fish Creek with perennial flow, site A-RB, the streambed substrate in Fish Creek contained primarily cobble in the size range of 64 to <128 mm, and gravel in the size range of 32 to <64 mm, with a few boulders and some fine sediment (fig. 26). The streambed substrate at site A-RB was dominated by gravel in the size range of 8 to <64 mm. The differences in substrate size between site A-RB and the downstream sites on Fish Creek likely are due, at least partially, to the increased streamflow at sites farther downstream.

Comparison of substrate before and after the peak flow of 2008 showed little difference between the two time periods. One exception was site A-RB, which showed an increase in fines in October; however, this is likely due to a summer 2008 landslide into the creek in Phillips Canyon, a tributary of Fish Creek, rather than a function of changing flow conditions in Fish Creek.

Riparian Canopy

Densiometer readings were recorded in October 2008 at sites A-RB, A-R3D, A-Wck, A-R6D, and A-R7 (table 2) as an indicator of riparian canopy cover and shading that might limit light availability for photosynthesis by the aquatic plant communities. The average riparian canopy cover ranged from 0 percent at site A-R7 to 59 percent at site A-Wck (table 20). Site A-Wck had the highest amount of riparian canopy, but most of the stream channel still received full sunlight because of the width of the channel and the relatively short height of the riparian vegetation.

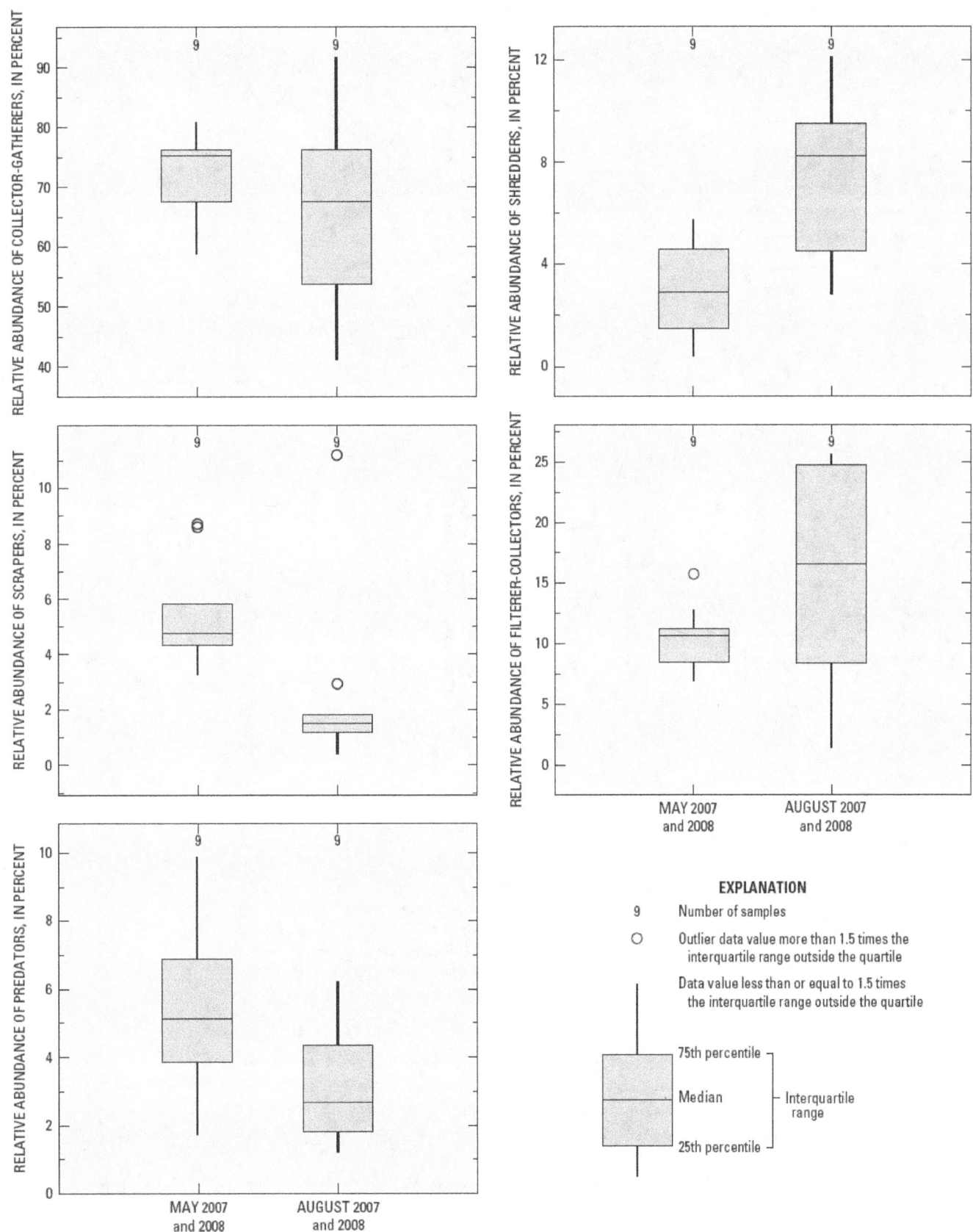

Figure 24. Relative abundance of functional feeding groups of macroinvertebrates at sites with perennial flow, Fish Creek, Wyoming, May and August, 2007–08.

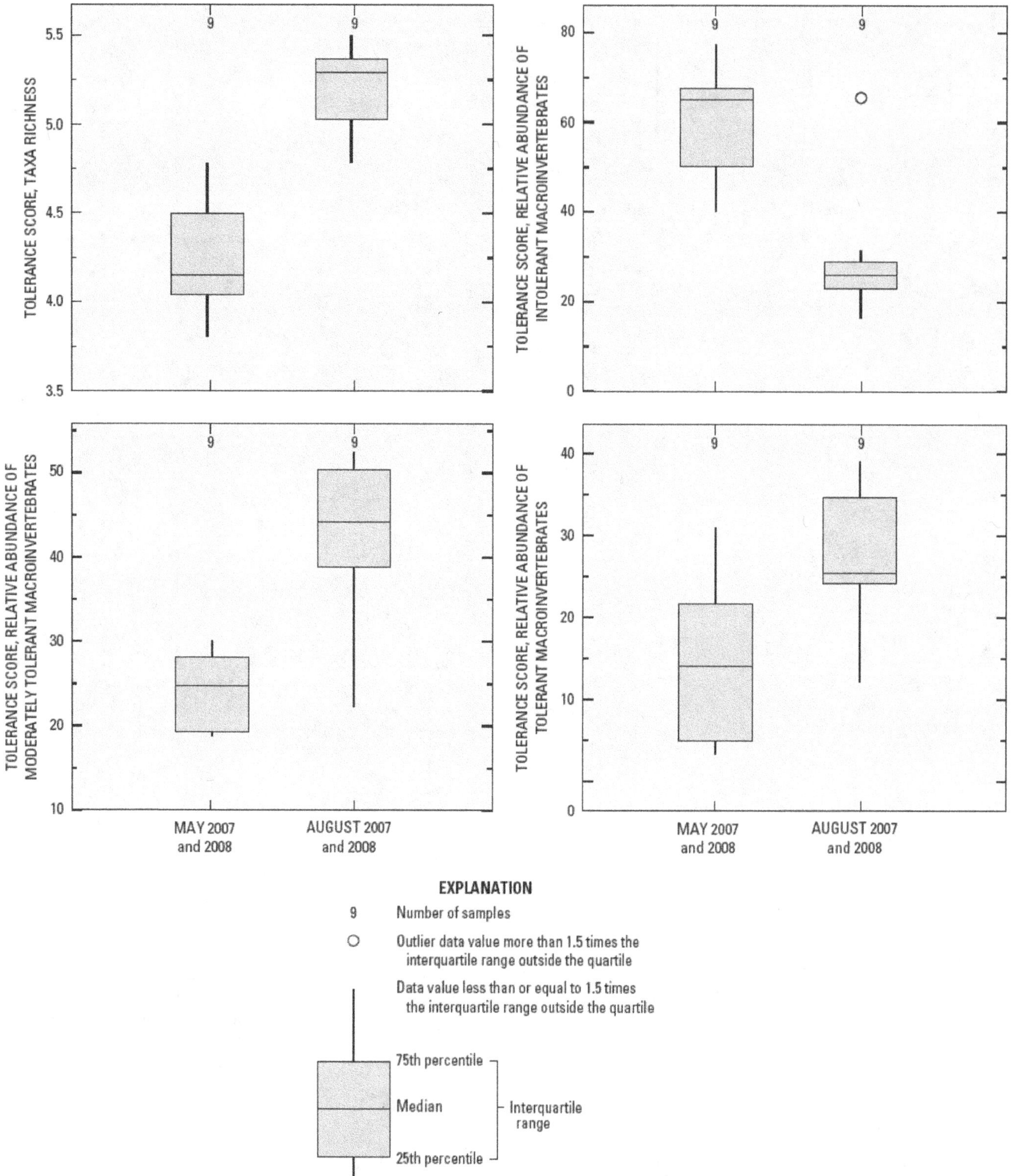

Figure 25. Tolerance scores for macroinvertebrate communities based on taxa richness and relative abundance for sites with perennial flow, Fish Creek, Wyoming, May and August, 2007–08.

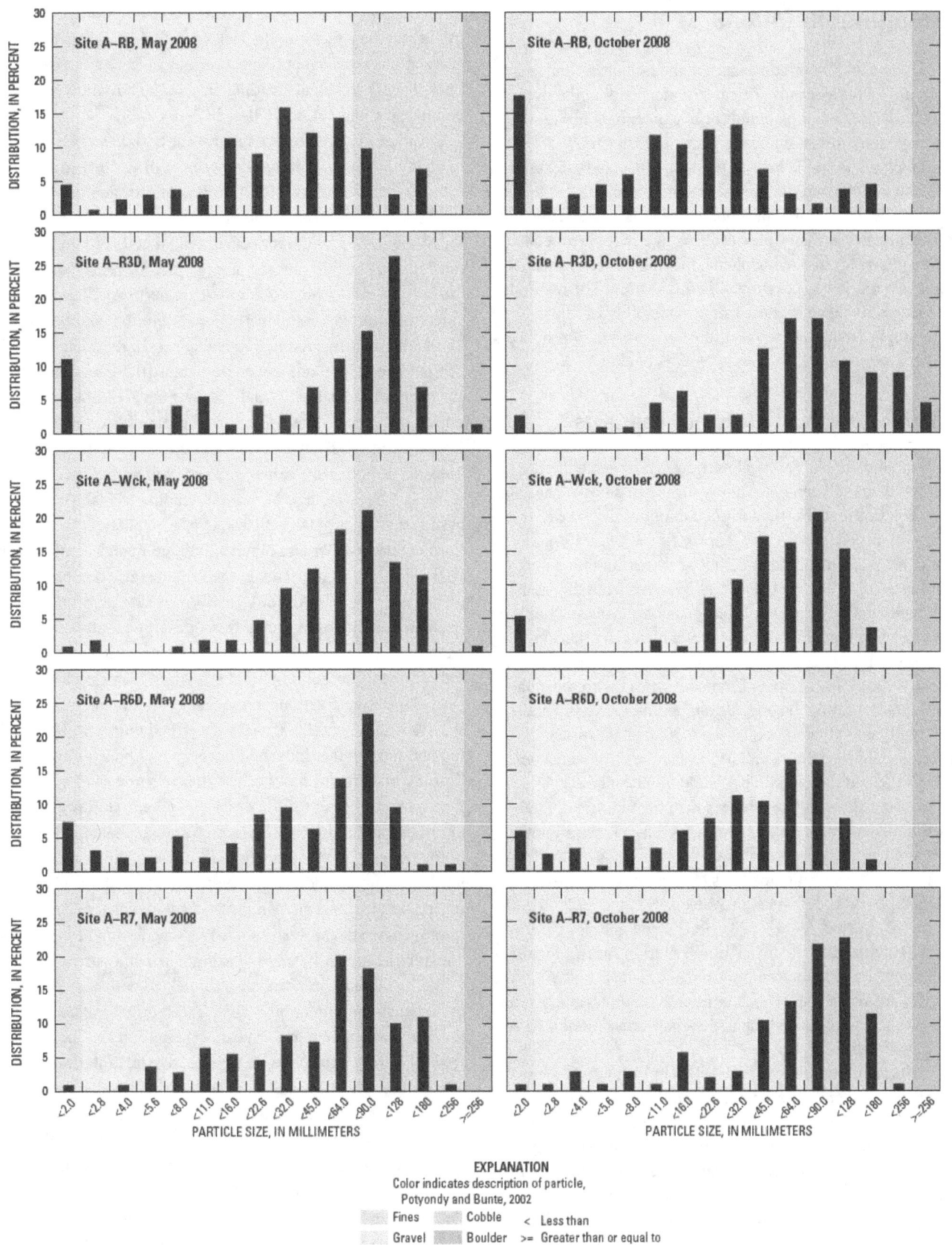

Figure 26.   Streambed substrate at five sites with perennial flow on Fish Creek, May and October, 2008

Ecological Relations

Understanding relations among the organisms and their environment (ecology) is critical to understanding the dynamics of Fish Creek and planning for any potential measures to control the growth of aquatic plants in Fish Creek. The aquatic plants form the base of the food chain and affect the macroinvertebrate communities, which in turn affects the fish communities. Given that the cobble and large gravel substrates and clear water in Fish Creek provide an environment conducive to growth of aquatic plants, the link between aquatic plants and nutrients is examined in this section. The relations are focused on algae because of the availability of relevant literature, but macrophytes also function as primary producers in Fish Creek.

Relations Between Algae and Nutrients

Aquatic criteria for algal nutrients (nitrogen and phosphorus) have not been determined for the State of Wyoming; therefore, nutrient criteria designed to minimize excessive algal growth, including *Cladophora*, on the Clark Fork in Montana (Watson and others, 2000) are used in this report for reference. All of the Fish Creek samples from the sites with perennial flow had total nitrogen concentrations (table 3) that were less than the unfiltered, total nitrogen criterion of 0.30 mg/L as N established for Clark Fork (Watson and others, 2000). Two samples from site A-R1U with seasonal flow had total nitrogen concentrations (unfiltered; 0.7 and 0.33 mg/L as N) that exceeded the 0.30 mg/L nitrogen criterion (table 3). Almost all of the samples from sites on Fish Creek with perennial flow had total phosphorus concentrations (unfiltered) that were less than the unfiltered, total phosphorus criterion of 0.039 mg/L as P as an overall upper limit and less than the criterion of 0.020 mg/L as P as a lower limit where the specific goal was to discourage the growth of *Cladophora* as described in Watson and others (2000). All samples from sites A-R1U and A-R1D, and one sample from site A-RB exceeded the lower-limit criterion for *Cladophora* (0.020 mg/L as P); one sample from site A-R1U and all of the samples from site A-R1D had unfiltered total phosphorus concentrations that exceeded the upper-limit criterion of 0.039 mg/L as P (table 3).

Although nutrient concentrations in Fish Creek generally were low, the standing crop of algae in Fish Creek was high compared to other streams in the region and was within the range of nuisance conditions (Stevenson and others, 1996; U.S. Environmental Protection Agency, 2000; Watson and others, 2000). This apparent paradox has also been noted for other ecosystems (for example, Porter and others, 2001; Peterson and others, 2001) and can be explained by rapid consumption of nutrients by the aquatic community as soon as the nutrients

are introduced to the system. Rapid consumption of nutrients might also be a factor in the lack of statistically significant correlations between nutrients (various forms of nitrogen and phosphorus) and algal standing crop (algal biovolume, algal cell density, and chlorophyll-*a*) in Fish Creek.

Either nitrogen or phosphorus, or both have been shown to be the nutrient-limiting algal growth in various streams (Stevenson and others, 1996). Ratios of nitrogen to phosphorus concentrations (N:P) sometimes are used as an indicator of the limiting nutrient because algal cells utilize those nutrients in specific ratios. For example, Stevenson and others (1996) suggest ambient N:P ratios greater than 20:1 are considered P limited, less than 10:1 are N limited, and between 10 and 20 to 1, the distinction is unclear. In the surface waters of Fish Creek, N:P ratios were less than 10:1 at all sites in late summer and fall (fig. 27) and greater than 10:1 at some sites during the spring. The N:P ratios in groundwater in the Fish Creek area (fig. 27) were similar to those in the surface water, in terms of both ratio values and seasonal variation. Groundwater is a likely source of nutrient loading to Fish Creek, based on substantial contributions of groundwater to Fish Creek (Eddy-Miller and others, 2009) and consistently higher concentrations of nutrients in the groundwater compared to the surface water. Additional analyses would be needed to quantify loading of nutrients from groundwater to surface water and determine the function of groundwater in the potential nitrogen limitation of algal growth in Fish Creek.

Other investigations in the Rocky Mountain area such as Watson and others (2000) have described nutrient limitation to algal growth that indicated nitrogen and phosphorus were limiting at different times of the year in some river systems. Peterson and Porter (2001) described potential nitrogen limitation in the Yellowstone River in Montana. Also, N:P ratios in Fish Creek in late summer and fall were within the range used by Lohman and Priscu (1992) as an indicator of nitrogen limitation at stream sites in western Montana. The Federal Interagency Stream Restoration Working Group (1998) noted phosphorus typically is the limiting nutrient in streams.

The increase in nitrogen-fixing algae with season and in the downstream direction in Fish Creek might indicate that the nitrogen-fixing algae are using their ability to fix atmospheric nitrogen to achieve a competitive advantage over other algae when nitrogen concentrations in water are low. Concentrations of nitrogen in water showed a seasonal fluctuation and tended to be lowest in late summer and fall, when algal standing crop and production were high, as contrasted with concentrations of phosphorus in water that tended to be stable throughout the sampling period. Additional sampling and analysis would be required to determine whether nitrogen, phosphorus, or both are the primary nutrients responsible for growth of algae in Fish Creek.

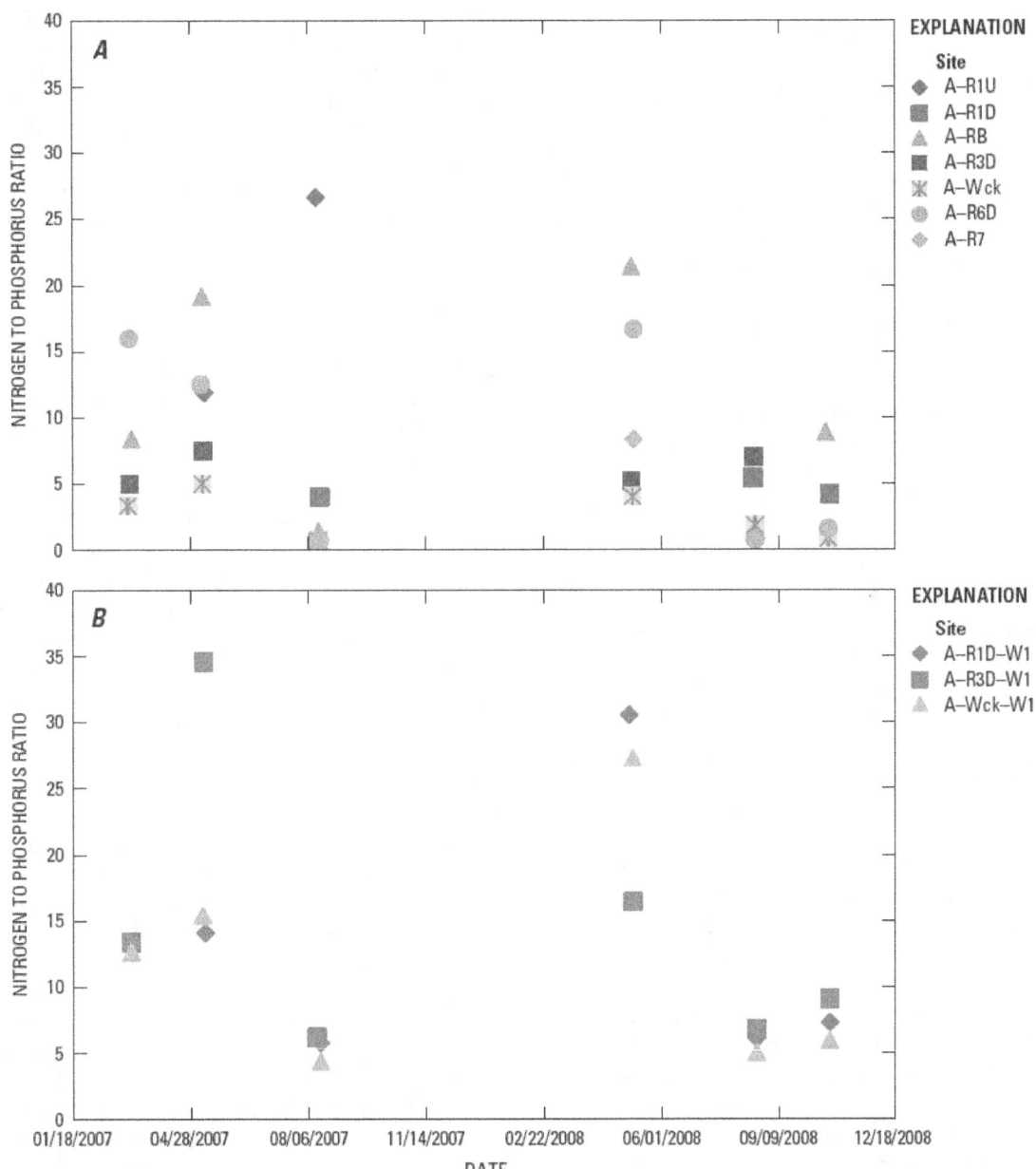

Figure 27. Ratios of nitrogen to phosphorus concentrations (N:P). *A,* surface-water samples, and *B,* groundwater samples, Fish Creek area, 2007–08.

Relations Between Aquatic Plants and Higher Trophic Levels

The aquatic plant communities in Fish Creek affect the macroinvertebrate and fish communities in various ways such as by providing food and shelter, as well as causing diel changes in dissolved-oxygen concentrations. In both 2007 and 2008, macroinvertebrate communities shifted seasonally, with higher proportions of Ephemeroptera, Plecoptera, and Trichoptera in May than in August, and higher proportions of Diptera and noninsects in August than May. The functional feeding

groups and tolerance scores of the macroinvertebrate communities also shifted seasonally. For example, relative abundance of the scraper feeding mode was significantly higher in May than August, whereas the shredder feeding mode was significantly higher in August and May. The seasonal changes in macroinvertebrate communities were consistent with the seasonal increases in *Cladophora* and macrophytes in Fish Creek that affect food and shelter available to the macroinvertebrates. The macroinvertebrates, in turn, are an important food source for the fish community that is dominated by salmonids, such as the Snake River cutthroat trout (*Oncorhynchus clarki* spp.).

Summary

Fish Creek, a tributary to the Snake River, is about 25 river kilometers long and is located in Teton County in western Wyoming near the town of Wilson. Nuisance growths of aquatic plants have been increasing in Fish Creek in recent years. To address this concern, the U.S. Geological Survey conducted a study in cooperation with the Teton Conservation District to characterize the water quality and biological communities in Fish Creek. Water-quality samples were collected for analyses of physical properties and water chemistry (nutrients, nitrate isotopes, and wastewater chemicals) between March 2007 and October 2008 from seven surface-water sites and three groundwater wells. During this same period, aquatic plant and macroinvertebrate samples were collected and habitat characteristics were measured at the surface-water sites.

The main objectives of this study were to (1) evaluate nutrient concentrations (that influence biological indicators of eutrophication) and potential sources of nutrients by using stable isotope analysis and other indicator chemicals (such as caffeine and disinfectants) that could provide evidence of anthropogenic sources, such as wastewater or septic tank contamination in Fish Creek and adjacent groundwater, and (2) characterize the algal, macrophyte, and macroinvertebrate communities and habitat of Fish Creek.

On the west side of the Snake River is an alluvial aquifer known locally as the west bank aquifer. Fish Creek's streambed is incised into the sediments of the Snake River alluvium and intersect the water table of the west bank aquifer. Groundwater discharge contributes a substantial portion of the flow to Fish Creek, although the volume of water contributed from groundwater varies along the length of the creek.

Seven surface-water and three groundwater sites were selected for sampling on the basis of their location along the reach of Fish Creek from near the headwaters at Teton Village to a location about 2 kilometers from the confluence with the Snake River. Physical properties were determined in the field for all surface-water and groundwater sites during each visit. Streamflow was measured at surface-water sites, and water-level data were collected at groundwater sites. Water-quality samples from Fish Creek and nearby groundwater were collected for analyses of nutrients, nitrate isotopes, and wastewater chemicals, depending on the sampling schedule. Biological samples (aquatic plants and macroinvertebrates) were collected and streambed substrate and riparian canopy were measured at all surface-water sites.

Nitrate was the dominant species of dissolved nitrogen present in all samples and was the only bioavailable species detected at concentrations greater than the laboratory reporting level in all surface-water samples. Average concentrations of dissolved nitrate in surface water were largest in samples collected from the two upstream sites with seasonal flow near Teton Village and decreased downstream with the smallest concentration at site A-Wck. Concentrations of dissolved nitrate in groundwater were consistently greater than concentrations in the corresponding surface-water sites during the same sampling event. Orthophosphate was the primary dissolved species of phosphorus present in all surface-water and groundwater samples. The average concentration of dissolved orthophosphate in surface water was largest (0.05 milligram per liter [mg/L] as phosphorus) in samples collected near Teton Village; samples from all other sites had equal average concentrations of 0.01 mg/L as phosphorus. Concentrations of dissolved orthophosphate in groundwater typically were greater than concentrations in the corresponding surface-water sites during the same sampling event.

When viewed from the shore or a bridge, Fish Creek commonly appeared to be bright green due to a green mat of aquatic plants on the bottom of the creek. The mat typically was composed of a mixture of macrophytes, macroalgae, microalgae, and moss. The composition of the aquatic plant community in Fish Creek appeared to shift in the downstream direction in 2007. The downstream increase in macrophytes was accompanied by a downstream decrease in microalgae. The proportion of the macroalgae *Cladophora* in the aquatic plant community was relatively high at sites A-Wck and A-R3D in both 2007 and 2008. *Cladophora* at site A-Wck made up an average of about 40 percent of the plant community in 2007 and 46 percent in 2008.

The relative abundance of macrophytes in the aquatic plant community generally increased from summer to fall at all of the sites with perennial flow during 2007 and at some of the sites during 2008. The seasonal increase in the proportion of macrophytes generally corresponded with decreases in the proportion of microalgae and unsuitable substrate, likely because the growth of macrophytes covered areas that would otherwise have been classified as microalgae or unsuitable substrate.

Concentrations of chlorophyll-*a*, which is one of the primary photosynthetic pigments in algal cells tended to be higher at the sites with perennial flow than at sites with seasonal flow. Chlorophyll-*a* concentrations at the two sampling sites farthest upstream, sites A-R1U and A-R1D with seasonal flow, were highly variable but averaged less than 200 milligrams per square meter (mg/m^2) in 2007. In contrast, chlorophyll-*a* concentrations at the sites with perennial flow, sites A-RB, A-R3D, A-Wck, and A-R6D, averaged greater than 200 mg/m^2. Average concentrations of chlorophyll-*a* were smallest in the spring months of March and May and largest in October 2007. The chlorophyll-*a* concentrations during 2008 also indicated a seasonal peak in October.

Concentrations of chlorophyll-*a* in Fish Creek consistently were high compared to values from other investigations. Almost all of the chlorophyll-*a* concentrations from Fish Creek were in the range of, or exceeded, the 100 to 200 mg/m^2 range suggested as an indicator of nuisance algal conditions by the U.S. Environmental Protection Agency.

Most of the 199 algal taxa identified in the 2007 samples were diatoms (Bacillariophyta), accounting for 87 percent of the total taxa richness by sample. In spite of having relatively few species, blue-green algae commonly were dominant in terms of density and green algae commonly were dominant in terms of biovolume at sites with perennial flow. The taxonomic composition of the algal communities at the sites with seasonal flow was notably different from the composition at sites with perennial flow.

Algal community traits were calculated from genus or species-level autecological information as potential indicators of nitrogen limitation, organic enrichment, sedimentation, and pH. Nitrogen-fixing algae were present and sometimes dominant in the algal communities of Fish Creek. Nitrogen-fixing algae include diatoms in the family Rhopalodiaceae and blue-green algae that can fix atmospheric nitrogen as a nutrient source and therefore have a competitive advantage when concentrations of nitrogen, a key nutrient for algae, in the water are low. Metrics for oxygen tolerance, organic nitrogen, and pollution class indicated relatively low organic enrichment in Fish Creek.

Similar to the algal communities, the macroinvertebrate taxa richness was lower at the sites with seasonal streamflow, A-R1U and A-R1D, near Teton Village than at the sites farther downstream with perennial flow, likely due to the effects of drying during the winter and differences in the food sources (algae, other aquatic plants, and organic matter). The Diptera (true flies) made up about one-half of the macroinvertebrate taxa identified in Fish Creek. The Ephemeroptera (mayflies), Trichoptera (caddisflies), and Plecoptera (stoneflies), which are collectively known as the EPT, accounted for smaller proportions of the overall community taxa richness than Diptera and were more common in May than August of both 2007 and 2008, indicating seasonal variation in community composition Generally, the EPT are considered indicators of favorable water quality, and their proportions decrease in response to increasing perturbation. The proportion of organisms tolerant of degraded water quality, such as many of the Diptera and noninsects, is expected to increase with increasing perturbation. Although the seasonal change in macroinvertebrate community composition in Fish Creek indicates a shift toward more tolerant taxa later in the year, this change might be due to factors other than water quality, such as the change in algal communities.

In general, the streambed substrate consisted primarily of gravel and cobbles, with few boulders and some fine sediment. Riparian canopy measurements indicated minimal, if any, shading along the creek. The cobble and large gravel substrates and clear water in Fish Creek provide an environment conducive to growth of aquatic plants.

Although nutrient concentrations in Fish Creek generally were low, the standing crop of algae in Fish Creek was high compared to other streams in the region, and was within the range of nuisance conditions. This apparent paradox has also been noted in other ecosystems and can be explained by rapid consumption of nutrients by the aquatic community as soon as the nutrients are introduced to the system. Rapid consumption of nutrients also might be a factor in the lack of statistically significant correlation between nutrients (various forms of nitrogen and phosphorus) and algal standing crop (algal biovolume, algal cell density, and chlorophyll-a concentrations) in Fish Creek.

Ratios of nitrogen to phosphorus concentrations (N:P) sometimes are used as an indicator of the limiting nutrient because algal cells utilize those nutrients in specific ratios. Ambient N:P ratios greater than 20:1 are considered phosphorus limited, less than 10:1 are considered nitrogen limited, and between 10 and 20 to 1, the distinction is unclear. In the surface waters of Fish Creek, N:P ratios were less than 10:1 at all sites in late summer and fall and greater than 10:1 at some sites during the spring. The N:P ratios in groundwater in the Fish Creek area were similar to those in the surface water, in terms of both ratio values and seasonal variation.

The increase in nitrogen-fixing algae with season and in the downstream direction in Fish Creek might indicate that the nitrogen-fixing algae are using their ability to fix atmospheric nitrogen to achieve a competitive advantage over other algae when nitrogen concentrations in water are low. Concentrations of nitrogen in water showed a seasonal fluctuation and tended to be lowest in late summer and fall, when algal standing crop and production were high, as contrasted with concentrations of phosphorus in water that tended to be stable throughout the sampling period. Additional sampling and analysis would be required to determine whether nitrogen, phosphorus, or both, are the primary nutrients causing the growth of algae in Fish Creek.

The aquatic plant communities in Fish Creek affect the macroinvertebrate and fish communities in various ways such as by providing food and shelter, and causing diel changes in dissolved oxygen. In both 2007 and 2008, macroinvertebrate communities shifted seasonally, with higher proportions of Ephemeroptera, Plecoptera, and Trichoptera in May than in August, and higher proportions of Diptera and noninsects in August than May. The functional feeding groups and tolerance scores of the macroinvertebrate communities also shifted seasonally. For example, relative abundance of the scraper feeding mode was significantly higher in May than August, whereas the shredder feeding mode was significantly higher in August and May. The seasonal changes in macroinvertebrate communities were consistent with the seasonal increases in *Cladophora* and macrophytes in Fish Creek that affect food and shelter available to the macroinvertebrates. The macroinvertebrates, in turn are an important food source for the fish community that is dominated by salmonids, such as the Snake River cutthroat trout (*Oncorhynchus clarki* spp.).

References Cited

Bahls, L.L., 1993, Periphyton assessment methods for Montana streams: Helena, Mont., Water Quality Bureau, Department of Health and Environmental Services, 69 p.

Barbour, M.T., Gerritsen, J., Snyder, B.D., and Stribling, J.B., 1999, Rapid bioassessment protocols for use in streams and wadeable rivers—Periphyton, benthic macroinvertebrates, and fish (2d ed.): U.S. Environmental Protection Agency, Office of Water, EPA 841-B-99-002, variable pagination.

Baxter, G.T., and Stone, M.D., 1995, Fishes of Wyoming: Cheyenne, Wyoming Game and Fish Department Bulletin no. 4, 290 p.

Bott, T.L., 2006, Primary productivity and community respiration, *in* Hauer, F.R., and Lamberti, G.A., eds., Methods in stream ecology: Oxford, U.K., Elsevier Inc., 877 p.

Bray, J.R., and Curtis, J.T., 1957, An ordination of the upland forest communities of southern Wisconsin: Ecological Monographs, v. 27, p. 325–349.

Case, J.C., Arneson, C.S., and Hallberg, L.L., 2000, Preliminary 1:500,000-scale digital surficial geology map of Wyoming: Wyoming State Geological Survey Digital Product HSDM 98-1.

Casciotti, K.L., Sigman, D.M., Galanter Hastings, M., Böhlke, J. K., and Hilkert, A., 2002, Measurement of the oxygen isotopic composition of nitrate in seawater and freshwater using the denitrifier method: Analytical Chemistry, v. 74, p. 4905–4912.

Charles, D.F., Knowles, C., and Davis, R.S., 2002, Protocols for the analysis of algal samples collected as part of the U.S. Geological Survey National Water-Quality Assessment Program: Philadelphia, Penn., Academy of Natural Sciences, Report 02-06, 124 p.

Childress, C.J.O., Foreman, W. T, Connor, B.F., and Maloney, T.J, 1999, New reporting procedures based on long-term method detection levels and some considerations for interpretations of water-quality data provided by the U.S. Geological Survey National Water Quality Laboratory: U.S. Geological Survey Open-File Report 99-193, 19 p.

Clark, I.D., and Fritz, Peter, 1997, Environmental isotopes in hydrogeology: New York, Lewis Publishers, 328 p.

Clark, M.L., Wheeler, J.D., and O'Ney, S.E., 2007, Water-quality characteristics of Cottonwood Creek, Taggart Creek, Lake Creek, and Granite Creek, Grand Teton National Park, Wyoming, 2006: U.S. Geological Survey Scientific Investigations Report 2007-5221, 44 p.

Clarke, K.R., and Gorley, R.N., 2006, PRIMER v6—User manual/tutorial: Plymouth, U.K., PRIMER-E-Ltd, 190 p.

Cox, E.R., 1974, Water resources of Grand Teton National Park, Wyoming: U.S. Geological Survey Open-File Report 74-1019, 114 p.

Cuffney, T.F., 2003, User's manual of the National Water-Quality Assessment Program invertebrate data analysis system (IDAS) software: U.S. Geological Survey Open-File Report 03-172, 103 p.

Eddy-Miller, C.A., Wheeler, J.D., and Essaid, H.I., 2009, Characterization of interactions between surface water and near-stream groundwater along Fish Creek, Teton County, Wyoming, by using heat as a tracer: U.S. Geological Survey Scientific Investigations Report 2009-5160, 53 p.

Fairchild, G.W., Lowe, R.L., and Richardson, W.B., 1985, Nutrient-diffusing substrates as an in situ bioassay using periphyton—Algal growth responses to combinations of N and P: Ecology, v. 66, p. 465–472.

Federal Interagency Stream Restoration Working Group, 1998, Stream corridor restoration—Principles, processes, and practices: GPO Item No. 0120-A, SuDocs No. A 57.6/2:EN 3/PT.653, variable pagination.

Fishman, M.J., ed., 1993, Methods of analysis by the U.S. Geological Survey National Water Quality Laboratory—Determination of inorganic and organic constituents in water and fluvial sediments: U.S. Geological Survey Open-File Report 93-125, 217 p.

Fitzpatrick, F.A., Waite, I.R., D'Arconte, P.J., Meador, M.R., Maupin, M.A., and Gurtz, M.E., 1998, Revised methods for characterizing stream habitat in the National Water-Quality Assessment Program: U.S. Geological Survey Water-Resources Investigations Report 98-4052, 67 p.

Graham, L.E., and Wilcox, L.W., 2000, Algae: Upper Saddle River, New Jersey, Prentice Hall, 640 p.

Helsel, D.R., and Hirsch, R.M., 1992, Statistical methods in water resources: Amsterdam, Elsevier Science Publishers, 529 p.

Hilsenhoff, W.L., 1987, An improved index of organic stream pollution: Great Lakes Entomologist, v. 20, p. 31–39.

Hinckley Consulting and Jorgensen Engineering, 1994, Groundwater impacts of residential ponds west of the Snake River: Teton County, Wyo., Hinckley Consulting and Jorgensen Engineering Report, 54 p.

Hynes, H.B.N., 1970, The ecology of running waters: Liverpool, Great Britain, Liverpool University Press, 555 p.

Kendall, Carol, and McDonnell, J.J., 1998, Isotope tracers in catchment hydrology: New York, Elsevier Publishers, 839 p.

Koterba, M.T., 1998, Ground-water data-collection protocols and procedures for the National Water-Quality Assessment Program—Collection, documentation, and compilation of required site, well, subsurface, and landscape data for wells: U.S. Geological Survey Water-Resources Investigations Report 98–4107, 91 p.

Lohman, Kirk, and Priscu, J.C., 1992, Physiological indicators of nutrient deficiency in *Cladophora* (Chlorophyta) in the Clark Fork of the Columbia River, Montana: Journal of Phycology, v. 48, no. 4, p. 443–448.

Love, J.D., and Christiansen, A.C., 1985, Geologic map of Wyoming: U.S. Geological Survey Geological map, scale 1:500,000, 3 sheets.

Love, J.D., Reed J.C., Jr., and Christiansen, A.C., 1992, Geologic map of Grand Teton National Park: U.S. Geological Survey Miscellaneous Investigations Series Map I–2031, scale 1:62,500.

Love, J.D., Reed, J.C., Jr., and Pierce, K.L., 2003, A geological chronicle of Jackson Hole and the Teton Range: Moose, Wyo., Grand Teton Natural History Association in cooperation with U.S. National Park Service, 132 p.

Merritt, R.W., and Cummins, K.W., eds., 1996, An introduction to the aquatic insects of North America, 3d ed.: Dubuque, Iowa, Kendall/Hunt Publishing Co., 862 p.

Moulton, S. R. II, Kennen, J.G., Goldstein, R.M., and Hambrook, J.A., 2002, Revised protocols for sampling algal, invertebrate, and fish communities as part of the National Water-Quality Assessment Program: U.S. Geological Survey Open-File Report 02–150, 75 p.

National Climatic Data Center, 2009, COOP Data/Record of Climatological Observations, U.S., data for station no. 486428, Moose, Wyo., accessed May 24, 2009, at *http://www.ncdc.noaa.gov/oa/mpp/*.

Natural Resources Conservation Service, 2008, Wyoming monthly precipitation averages (1971–2000): Natural Resources Conservation Service, National Water and Climate Center, data for Wyoming, Phillips Bench SnoTel, accessed December 1, 2008, at *http://www.wcc.nrcs.usda. gov/ snow/30yrprec.html*.

Nelson Engineering, 1992, Teton County westbank ground-water study: Jackson, Wyo., Nelson Engineering Report, 61 p.

Nolan, B.T., Campbell, D.L., and Senterfit, R.M., 1998, Depth of the base of the Jackson aquifer, based on geophysical exploration, southern Jackson Hole, Wyoming, USA: Springer-Verlag Hydrogeology Journal, v. 6, p. 374–382.

Nolan, B.T., and Miller, K.A., 1995, Water resources of Teton County, Wyoming, exclusive of Yellowstone Nation Park: U.S. Geological Survey Water-Resources Investigations Report 95–4204, 76 p.

Odum, H.T., 1956, Primary production in flowing waters: Limnology and Oceanography, v. 1, no. 2, p. 102–117.

Oregon Climate Service, 2010, Average annual precipitation, 1971–2000, Wyoming: Corvallis, Oregon State University, Oregon Climate Service, digital data, accessed August 18, 2010, at *http://www.prism.oregonstate.edu/pub/prism/ state_ppt/wyoming.png*.

Patton, C.J., and Kryskalla, J.R., 2003, Methods of analysis by the U.S. Geological Survey National Water Quality Laboratory—Evaluation of alkaline persulfate digestion as an alternative to Kjeldahl digestion for determination of total and dissolved nitrogen and phosphorus in water: U.S. Geological Survey Water-Resources Investigations Report 03–4174, 33 p.

Pennak, R.W., 1978, Freshwater invertebrates of the United States: New York, John Wiley and Sons, 803 p.

Peterson, C.G., and Grimm, N.B., 1992, Temporal variation in enrichment effects during periphyton succession in a nitrogen-limited desert stream ecosystem: Journal of the North American Benthological Society, v. 11, no. 1, p. 20–36.

Peterson, D.A., Porter, S.D., and Kinsey, S.M., 2001, Chemical and biological indicators of nutrient enrichment in the Yellowstone River Basin, Montana and Wyoming, August 2000—Study design and preliminary results: U.S. Geological Survey Water-Resources Investigation Report 2001–4238, 6 p.

Peterson, D.A., and Porter, S.D., 2002, Biological and chemical indicators of eutrophication in the Yellowstone River and major tributaries during August, 2000: National Water Quality Monitoring Council, Proceedings of the 2002 National Water Quality Monitoring Conference, Madison, Wisc., May 20–23, 14 p.

Porter, S.D., 2008, Algal attributes—An autecological classification of algal taxa collected by the National Water-Quality Assessment Program: U.S. Geological Survey Data Series 329, accessed August 8, 2010, at *http://pubs.usgs.gov/ds/ ds329/*.

Porter, S.D., Harris, M.A., and Kalkhoff, S.J., 2001, Influence of natural factors on quality of Midwestern streams and rivers: U.S. Geological Survey Water-Resources Investigations Report 2000–4288, 13 p.

Potyondy, John, and Bunte, Kristen, 2002, Sampling with US SAH-97 hand-held particle size analyzer: Federal Interagency Sedimentation Project, 6 p., accessed June 1, 2010, at *http://fisp.wes.army.mil/Instructions%20US_SAH-97_040412.pdf.*

Prescott, G.W., 1978, How to know the freshwater algae (3d ed.): Dubuque, Iowa, Wm. C. Brown Company Publishers, 293 p.

Rantz, S.E., and others, 1982, Measurement and computation of streamflow: U.S. Geological Survey Water-Supply Paper 2175, 2 v., 631 p.

Révész, Kinga, and Casciotti, Karen, 2007, Determination of the $\delta(^{15}N/^{14}N)$ and $\delta(^{18}O/^{16}O)$ of nitrate in water, RSIL Lab Code 2900, chap. C17 *of* Révész, Kinga, and Coplen, Tyler B., eds., Methods of the Reston Stable Isotope Laboratory: U.S. Geological Survey Techniques and Methods, book 10, sec. C, chap. 17, 24 p.

Sauer, V.B., 2002, Standards for the analysis and processing of surface-water data and information using electronic methods: U.S. Geological Survey Water-Resources Investigations Report 2001–4044, 91 p.

Sigman, D.M., Casciotti, K.L., Andreani, M., Barford, C., Galanter, M., and Böhlke, J.K., 2001, A bacterial method for the nitrogen isotopic analysis of nitrate in seawater and freshwater: Analytical Chemistry, v. 73, p. 4145–4153.

Sorenson, S.K., Porter, S.D., Akers, K.B., Harris, M.A., Kalkhoff, S.J., Lee, K.E., Roberts, L.R., and Terrio, P.J., 1999, Water quality and habitat conditions in upper Midwest streams relative to riparian vegetation and soil characteristics, August 1997—Study design, methods, and data: U.S. Geological Survey Open-File Report 99–202, 53 p.

Stevenson, R.J., Bothwell, M.L., and Lowe, R.L., 1996, Algal ecology—Freshwater benthic ecosystems: San Diego, Calif., Academic Press, 753 p.

Teply, M., and Bahls, L., 2007, Diatom biocriteria for Montana streams—Middle Rockies ecoregion, 2006: Helena, Montana Department of Environmental Quality, 14 p.

Timme, P.J., 1995, National Water Quality Laboratory 1995 Services Catalog: U.S. Geological Survey Open-File Report 95–352, 52 p.

U.S. Environmental Protection Agency, 2000, Nutrient criteria technical guidance manual, rivers and streams: EPA–822–B–00–002, 152 p.

U.S. Geological Survey, variously dated, National field manual for the collection of water-quality data: U.S. Geological Survey Techniques of Water-Resources Investigations, book 9, chaps. A1–A9, available on the Web, accessed December 14, 2009, at *http://water.usgs.gov/owq/FieldManual/.*

U.S. Geological Survey, 2009, National Water Information System, accessed December 29, 2009, at *http://waterdata.usgs.gov/nwis/annual.*

U.S. Geological Survey, 2010a, National Water Information System, accessed January 14, 2010, at *http://nwis.waterdata.usgs.gov/wy/nwis/.*

U.S. Geological Survey, 2010b, Characterization of Fish Creek—Groundwater/surface-water interaction, water quality, and aquatic biota, macroinvertebrate and algae data, accessed August 17, 2010, at *http://wy.water.usgs.gov/projects/fishcreek/data.htm.*

Van Dam, H., Mertens, A., and Sinkeldam, J., 1994, A coded checklist and ecological indicator values of freshwater diatoms from the Netherlands: Netherlands Journal of Aquatic Ecology, v. 28, no. 1, p. 117–133.

Watson, V.J., Ingman, G., and Anderson, B., 2000, Clark Fork River—Scientific basis of a nutrient TMDL for a river of the northern Rockies *in* Olsen, D.S., and Potyondy, J.P., eds., Wildland hydrology: Proceedings of an American Water Resources Association symposium, Bozeman, Mont., 1999, p. 67–74.

Wheeler, J.D., and Eddy-Miller, C.A., 2005, Seepage investigation on selected reaches of Fish Creek, Teton County, Wyoming, 2004: U.S. Geological Survey Scientific Investigations Report 2005–5133, 15 p.

Whitton, B.A., 1970, Biology of Cladophora in freshwaters: Water Research, v. 4, p. 457–476.

Wolman, M.G., 1954, A method for sampling coarse riverbed material: Transactions of the American Geophysical Union, v. 35, p. 951–956.

Wyoming State Engineer's Office, 2005, West bank Snake River hydrology study: Cheyenne, Wyoming State Engineer's Office Report, 92 p.

Zaugg, S.D., Smith, S.G., Schroeder, M.P., Barber, L.B., and Burkhardt, M.R., 2002, Methods of analysis by the U.S. Geological Survey National Water Quality Laboratory—Determination of wastewater compounds by polystyrene-divinylbenzene solid-phase extraction and capillary-column gas chromatography/mass spectrometry: U.S. Geological Survey Water-Resources Investigations Report 2001–4186, 37 p.

Supplemental Data

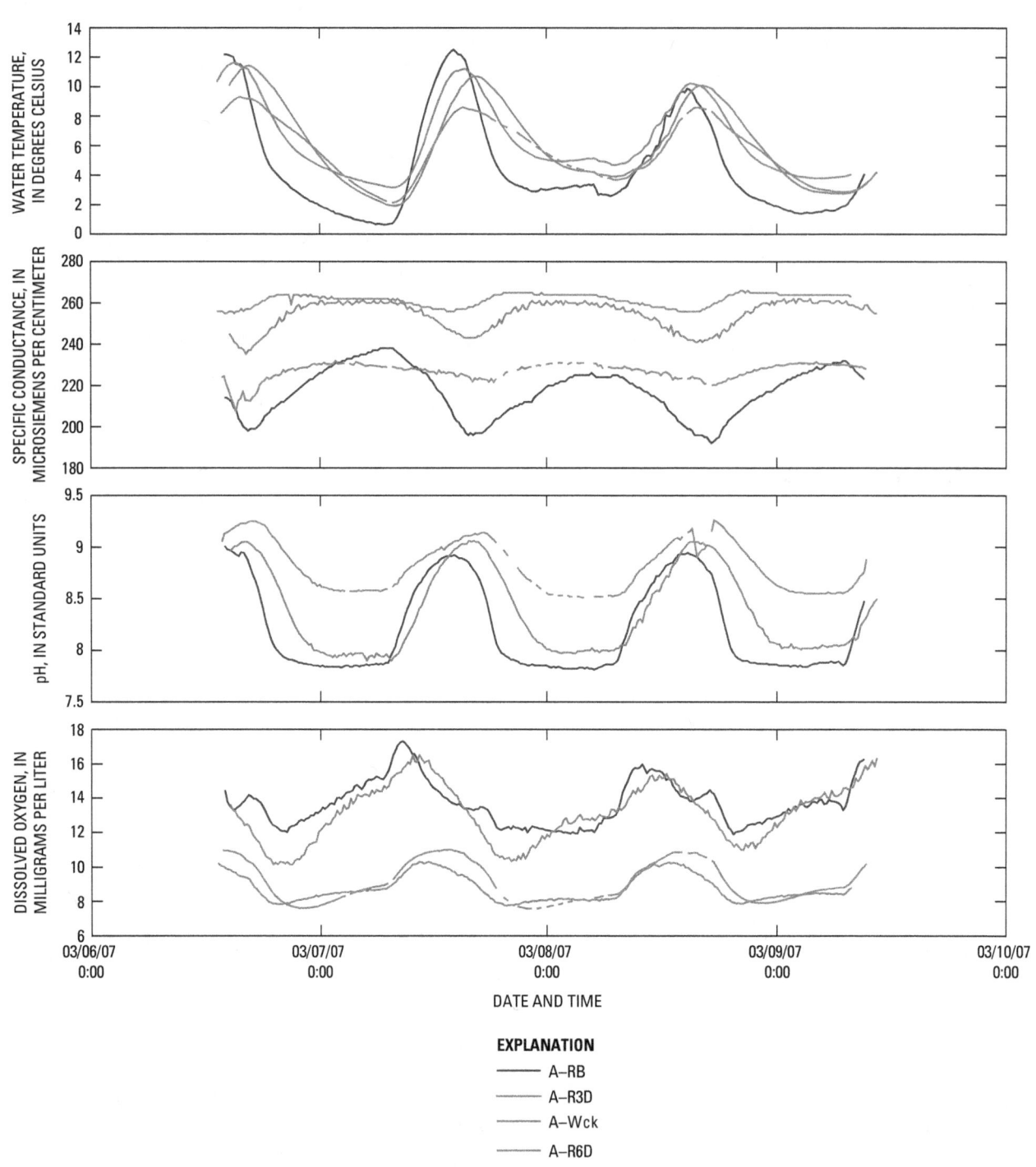

Figure 28.   Continuously collected measurements of water-quality properties from surface-water sites on Fish Creek, Wyoming, March 2007.

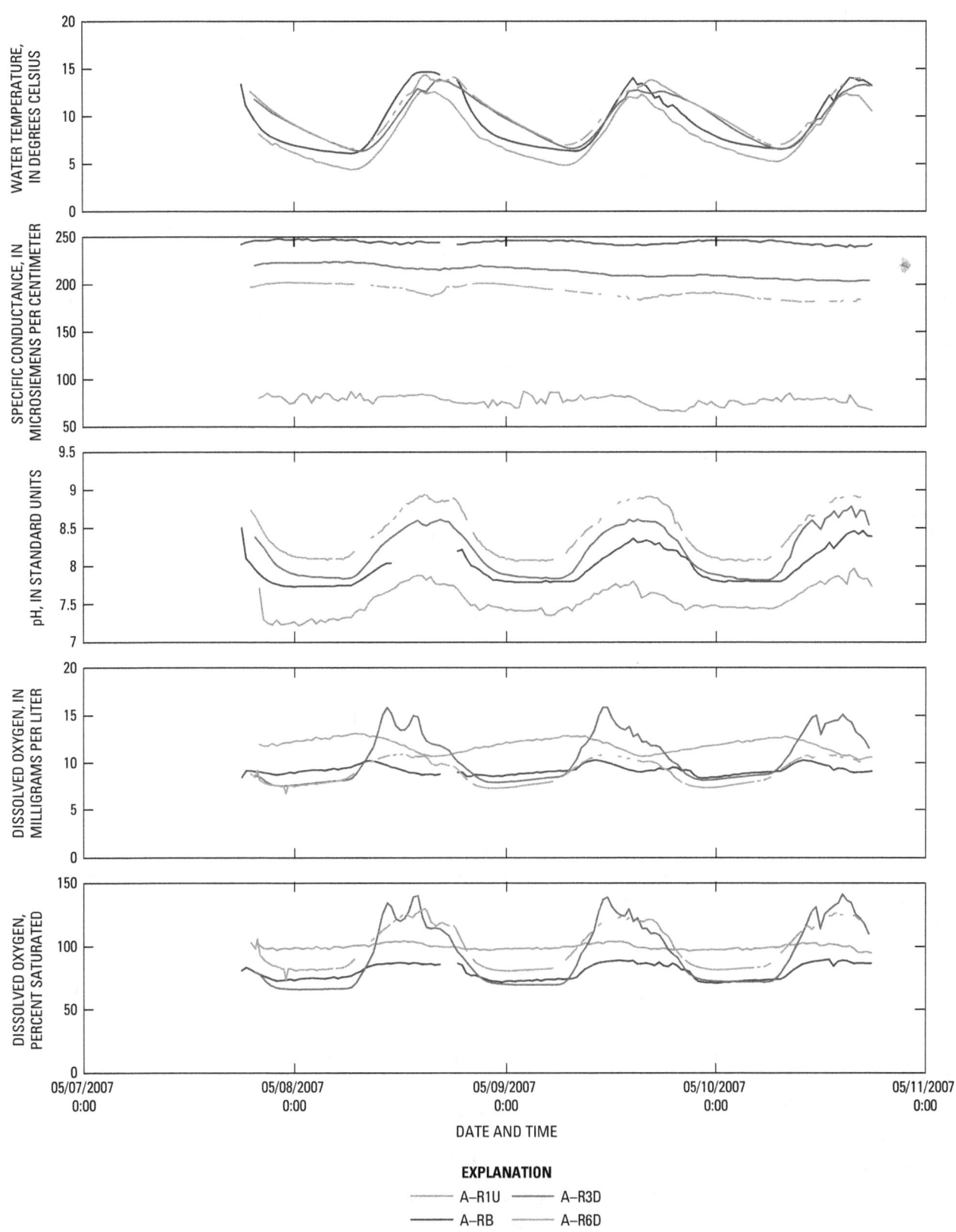

Figure 29. Continuously collected measurements of water-quality properties from surface-water sites on Fish Creek, Wyoming, May 2007.

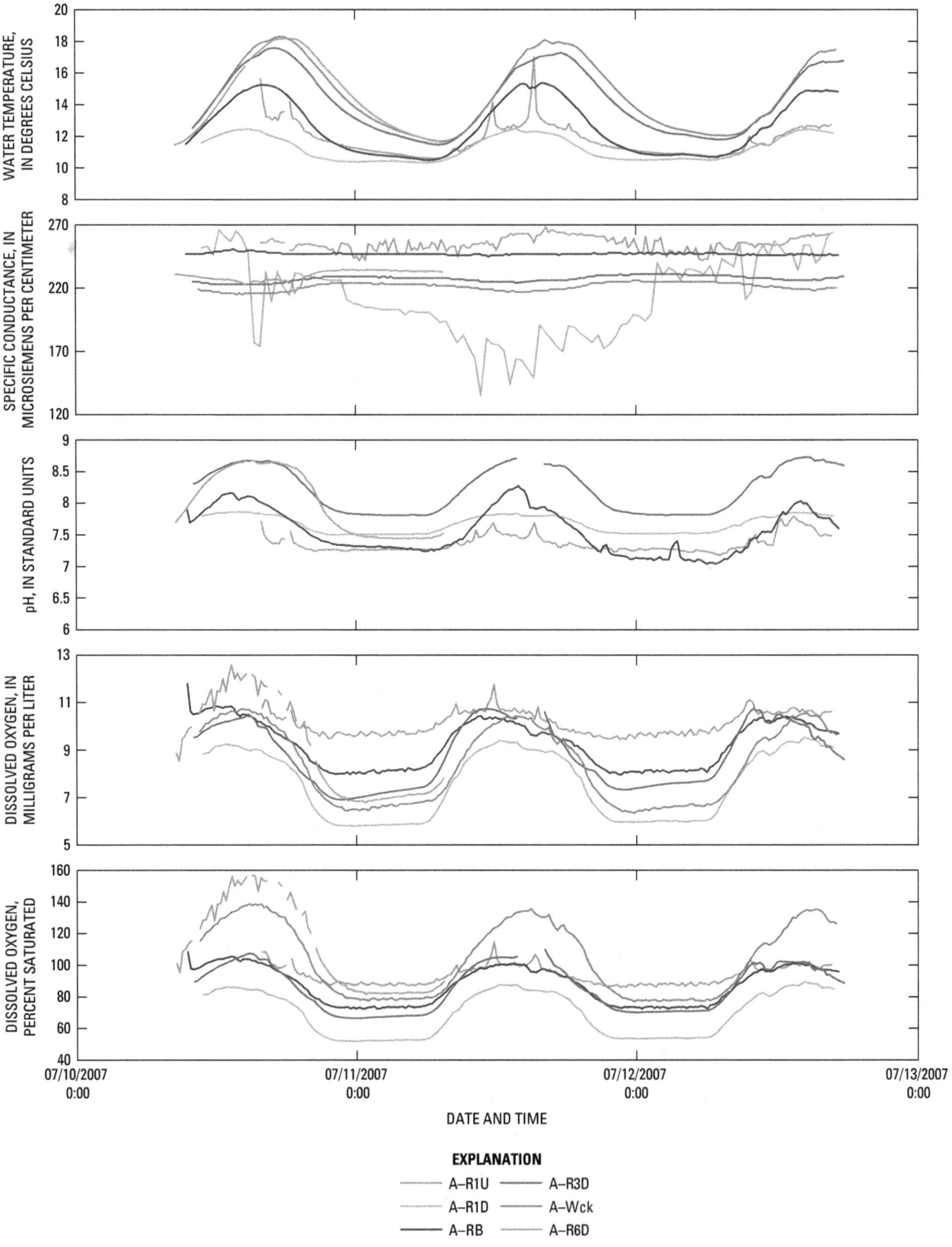

Figure 30. Continuously collected measurements of water-quality properties from surface-water sites on Fish Creek, Wyoming, July 2007.

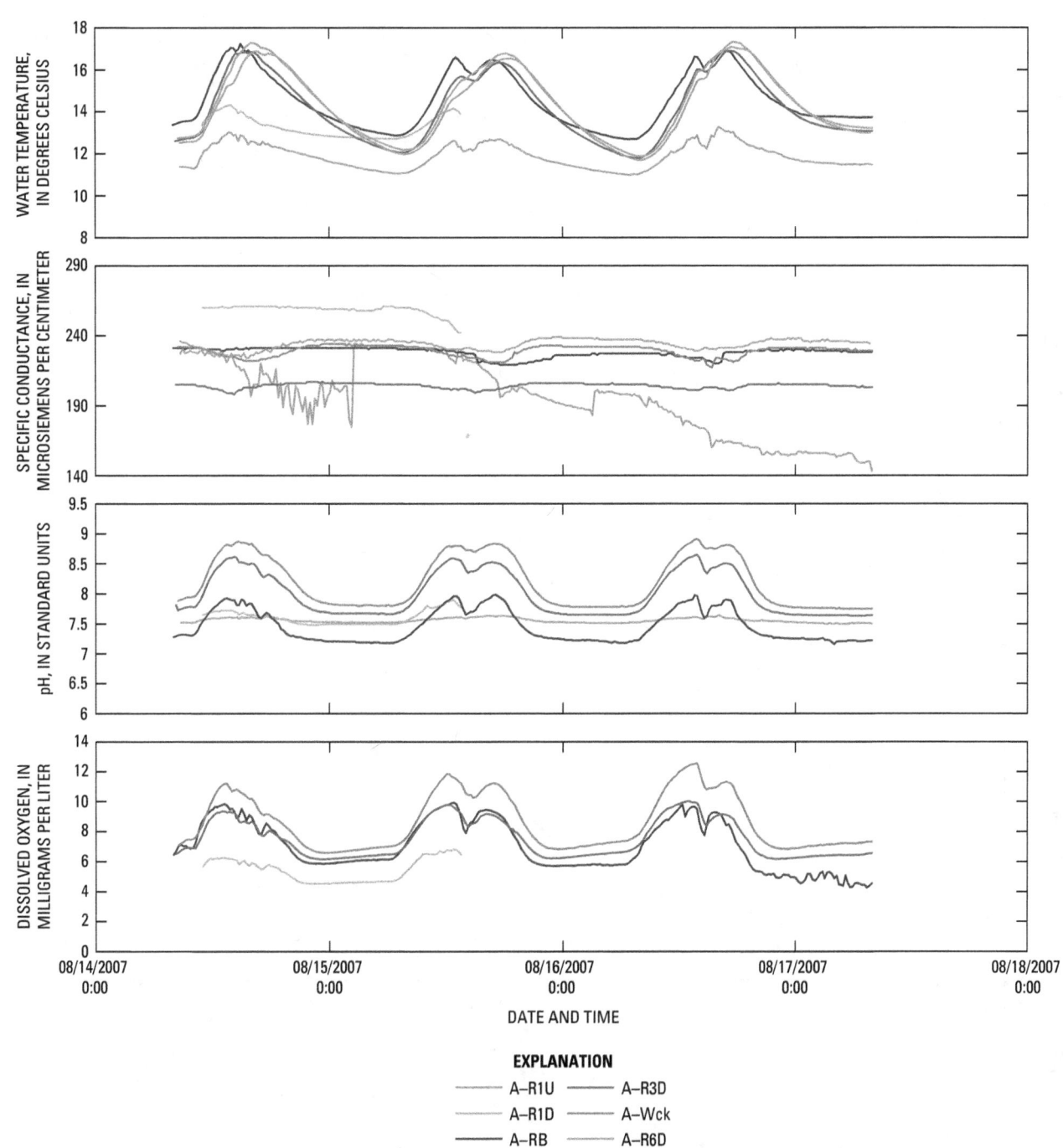

Figure 31. Continuously collected measurements of water-quality properties from surface-water sites on Fish Creek, Wyoming, August 2007.

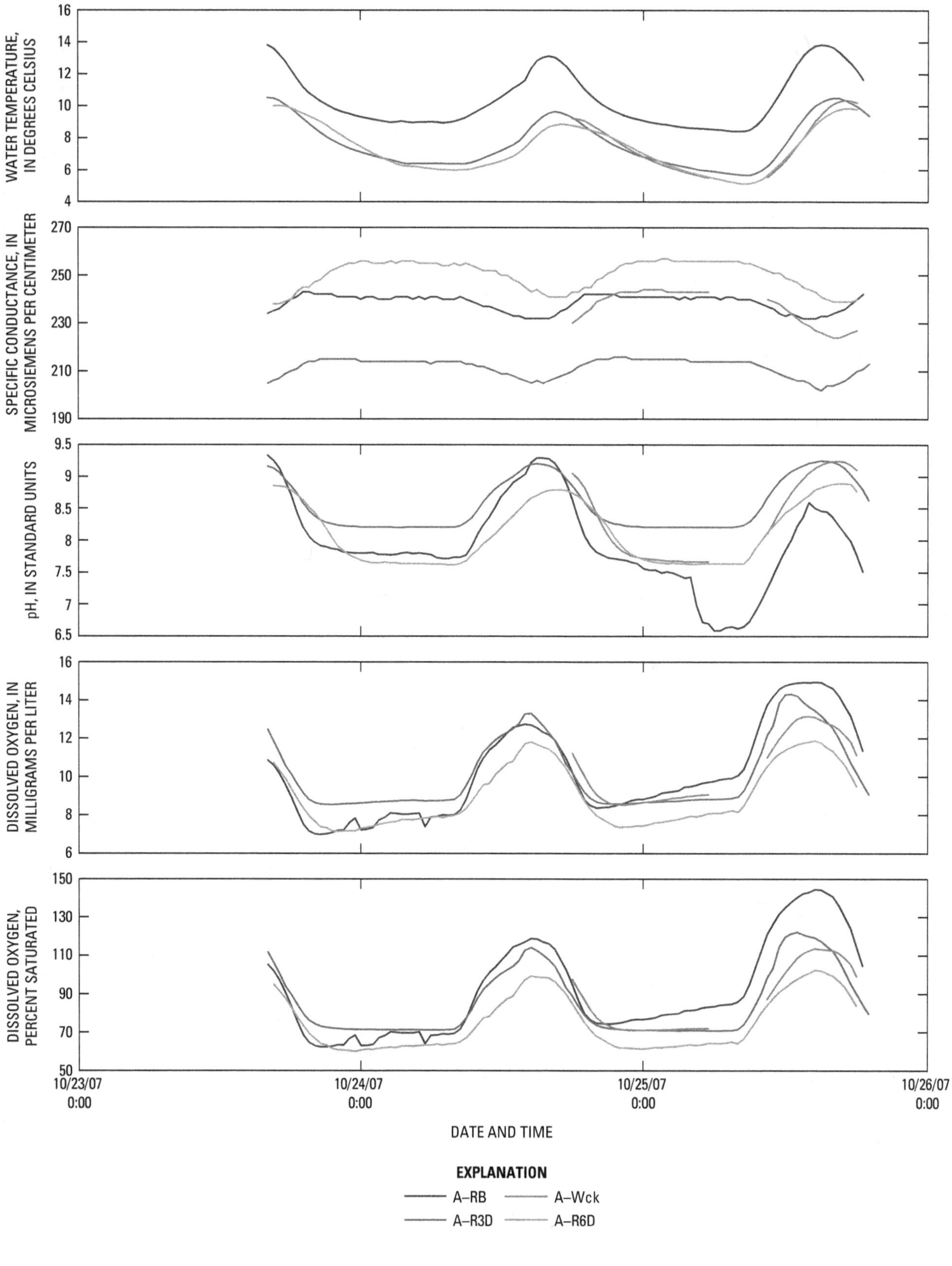

Figure 32. Continuously collected measurements of water-quality properties from surface-water sites on Fish Creek, Wyoming, October 2007.

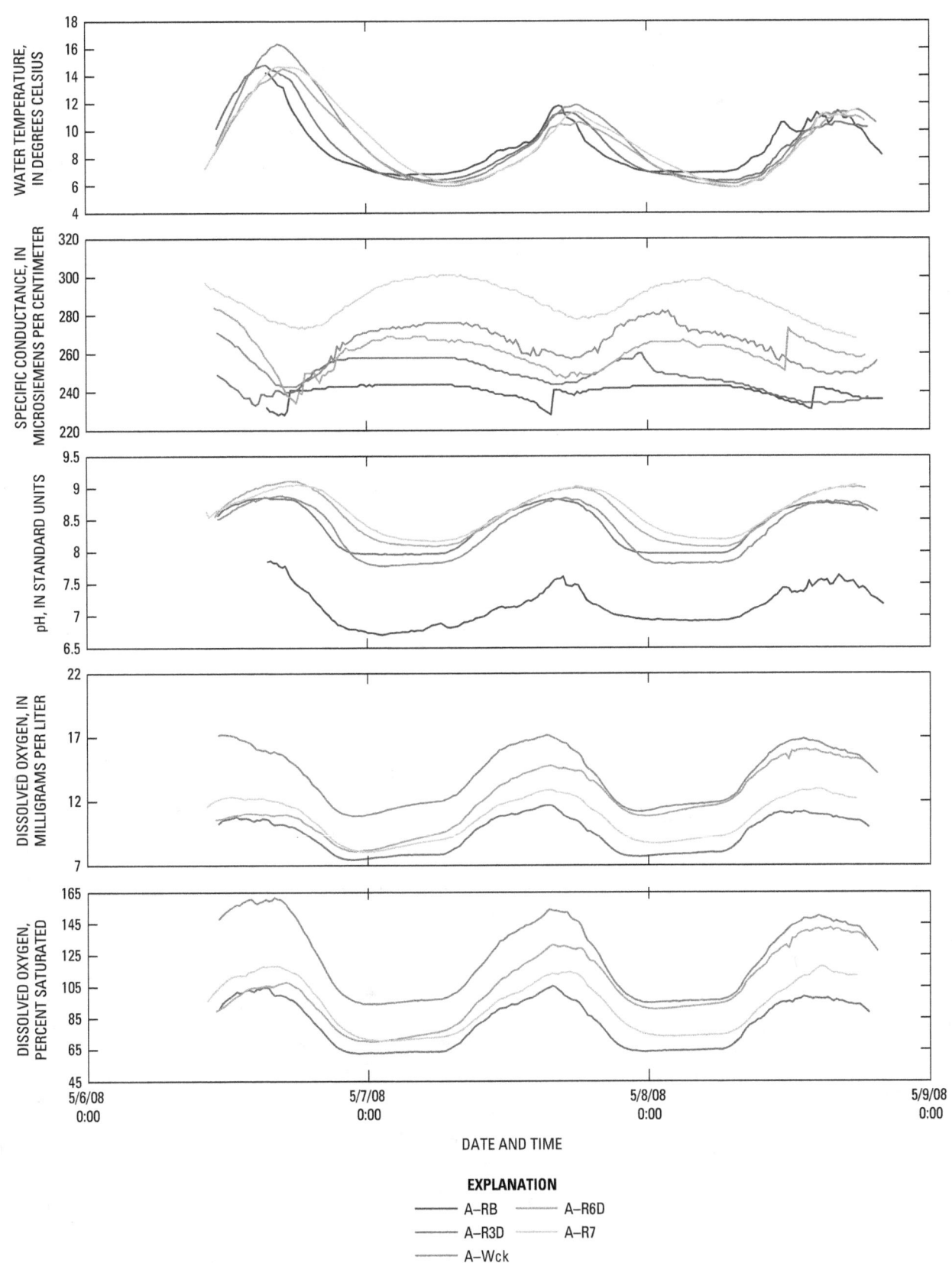

Figure 33. Continuously collected measurements of water-quality properties from surface-water sites on Fish Creek, Wyoming, May 2008

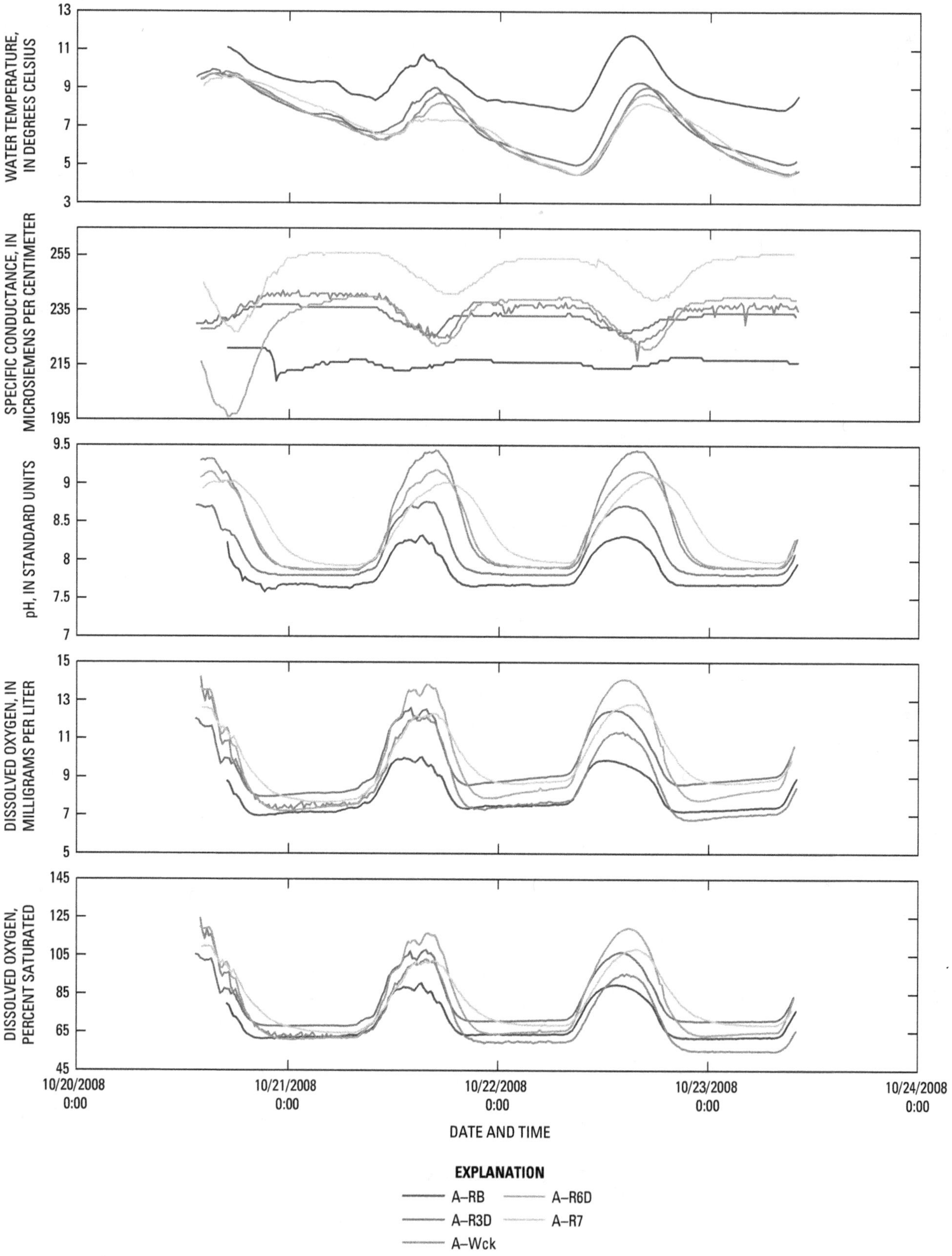

EXPLANATION

—— A–RB	—— A–R6D
—— A–R3D	······ A–R7
—— A–Wck	

Figure 34. Continuously collected measurements of water-quality properties from surface-water sites on Fish Creek, Wyoming, October 2008.

On CD–ROM in pocket at back of report:

Table 10.   Chemicals analyzed in the wastewater compound schedule (Zaugg and others, 2002).

Table 11.   Continuously collected measurements of water-quality properties from surface-water sites on Fish Creek, Wyoming, March 2007.

Table 12.   Continuously collected measurements of water-quality properties from surface-water sites on Fish Creek, Wyoming, May 2007.

Table 13.   Continuously collected measurements of water-quality properties from surface-water sites on Fish Creek, Wyoming, July 2007.

Table 14.   Continuously collected measurements of water-quality properties from surface-water sites on Fish Creek, Wyoming, August 2007.

Table 15.   Continuously collected measurements of water-quality properties from surface-water sites on Fish Creek, Wyoming, October 2007.

Table 16.   Continuously collected measurements of water-quality properties from surface-water sites on Fish Creek, Wyoming, May 2008.

Table 17.   Continuously collected measurements of water-quality properties from surface-water sites on Fish Creek, Wyoming, August 2008.

Table 18.   Continuously collected measurements of water-quality properties from surface-water sites on Fish Creek, Wyoming, October 2008.

Table 19.   Concentrations of wastewater chemicals in surface-water, groundwater, and associated blank samples collected in the Fish Creek area, 2007.

Table 20.   Densiometer readings from three cross sections at each surface-water site, October 2008.